GREAT AMERICAN ⬦ COOKING SCHOOLS

FOR
JAMES BEARD
AND JULIA CHILD,
WHO LIT THE LAMP
AND SHOWED US
THE WAY

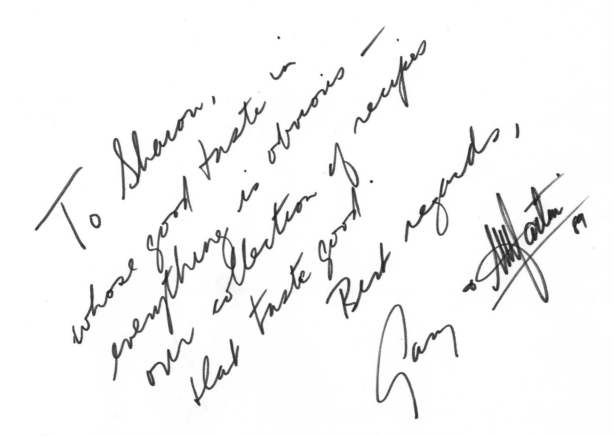

To Sharon,
whose good taste is obvious —
everything is obvious
own collection of recipes
that taste good.
Best regards,
Gary [signature] '89

If you would like to
receive a free color
catalog listing all our
books, please send your
name and address to:
Irena Chalmers Cookbooks, Inc.
P.O. Box 988, Denton, NC 27239.

GREAT AMERICAN COOKING SCHOOLS

Successful Parties

SIMPLE & ELEGANT

MARTIN JOHNER & GARY A. GOLDBERG

ILLUSTRATED BY ISADORE SELTZER

IRENA CHALMERS COOKBOOKS, INC. • NEW YORK

There are too many people to thank: our students and teachers who inspire us; our catering staff who make us proud; our office staff who hold us together. Our friends; families; supporters. Our clients, who prove the point that people who give parties are nice people.
Special thanks to Joanne Sugura and Gloria Benabo,
and to Bill and Boris for sharing them with us.

IRENA CHALMERS COOKBOOKS, INC.

PUBLISHER
Irena Chalmers

Sales and Marketing Director
Diane J. Robbins

Managing Editor
Jean Atcheson

Series Design
Helene Berinsky

Cover Design
Milton Glaser
Karen Skelton, *Associate Designer*

Cover Photography
Matthew Klein

Editor for this book
Jean Atcheson

Typesetting
Acu-Type Services, Clinton, CT

Printing
John D. Lucas Printing Co., Baltimore, MD

Editorial Offices
23 East 92nd Street
New York, NY 10128
(212) 289-3105

Sales Offices
P.O. Box 988
Denton, NC 27239
(800) 334-8128 or
(704) 869-4518 (NC)

ISBN #0-94-1034-19-4

© 1983 by Martin Johner and Gary A. Goldberg.
All rights reserved.
Printed and published in the United States of America
by Irena Chalmers Cookbooks, Inc.

**LIBRARY OF CONGRESS
CATALOG CARD NO.: 83-071040**
　Johner, Martin and Gary A. Goldberg.
　　Successful parties: simple and elegant.

　New York, NY: Chalmers, Irena Cookbooks, Inc.
84 p.
F G H I　　8 7 6 5　　595/18

Contents

Introduction

The largest party we have catered was for 3,000 people, the smallest, for a party of one. We feel safe in assuming that any party you have in mind will fall somewhere between these two extremes.

The extravaganza for 3,000 was in the courtyard of the Cloisters—a branch of The Metropolitan Museum of Art in Fort Tryon Park, high above the Hudson River. The event was part of their annual summer Medieval Festival, and we served sausages and cider, platters of cheeses and fruits, and whole-grain breads—all foods that were common during the Middle Ages in Europe. To carry the authenticity one step further, we wore the flowing white cotton robes of Franciscan monks. (These were borrowed for the occasion from a friend, a former Franciscan brother who lost the calling but kept the clothing.)

Our wursts and cider were so successful that, one week later, we moved our monks' show downtown to another outdoor festival, this time at the South Street Seaport Museum in Manhattan. Once again, sales were brisk, but our monks' robes—so charmingly authentic in the Gothic context of the Cloisters—now seemed like a misrepresentation. People called us "brother" and assumed that the proceeds of our sales were for the Franciscans. Needless to say, after a speedy donation at the nearest alms box, we retired the robes and wursts forever.

The party of one was the catalyst of our partnership. When Martin graduated from the Culinary Institute of America, he started a small and discreet private catering service in New York, and his ballotines and galantines soon became the rage among hostesses along Park Avenue. Martin's problem was that he couldn't say No, and when one of his clients cajoled him into giving a series of three consecutive dinners for a bedridden spouse—the party of one in question—it took him three solid days of cooking, and for very little profit. Good for the spouse, as they might say in Las Vegas, but not for the house.

Soon after this, I became Martin's business partner. This enabled him to channel his art and energy to the kitchen—the back of the house, as it is called—and I took responsibility for the contracts and the dining room—the front of the house. I also learned how to say No.

All of this happened over a dozen years ago, long before the "quicheing" of America—before the relish tray became crudité—and we have had great fun and success in riding the crest of the good-food wave that has swept across the country. Five years ago, we established Culinary Center of New York, in our firm belief that people wanted to learn from professionals how to cook well at home. We renovated a charming landmark Manhattan townhouse, complete with terraced garden, and so became at once a very well-appointed cooking school, and Manhattan's most unusual party place. Today we still cater many special events in our townhouse, as well as almost anywhere else where we are invited.

As our life and work are in New York City, we have, of course, catered for the rich and famous, and can name-drop with the best of them, and acceptance among the BPs (the Beautiful People) is good for our catering business and certainly flattering. However, our greatest source of pride lies in the wide acceptance and approval shown to us by a tougher crowd—the SFPs (the Serious Food People). These are the professionals in our business who know exactly what it takes to do what we do; we are grateful for their support.

This book is not intended to make you a professional caterer, nor would we trust any course of study for professional food preparation that is under two years in duration. What we've sought here is to help you make your party-giving at home delicious, simple and elegant. As two well-seasoned veterans, we pass the torch to you, with a nod and a wink: The key to a successful party is to make it all seem easy.

Yes, but how?

The Ten Rules of Party Giving

We think that parties should be fun, and so should party books. That said, tongue in chic but feet planted firmly on the ground, we present our Ten Rules of Party Giving.

1. READ THIS BOOK
(We don't know how you've managed without it.)

2. PLAN AHEAD AND ORGANIZE
Plan the budget, the type of party, the time, the guest list, the invitations, the menu (how to cook it, serve it, clean it) the bar, the staff, the music, the rentals, the flowers. Make charts and fill them in. Make lists and don't lose them. We'll help you with this in a page or two.

3. KEEP IT SIMPLE
A friend of ours—Bernie, the food groupie—remembers vividly the first "gourmet" party ever attempted by the love of his life. Down from the shelves came every classic French cookbook; out came every pot and pan. A hot soufflé, a cold mousse, perhaps a quenelle or two—ah, the raw courage of the novice chef. But while Bernie was luxuriating in a preprandial soak, there was a timid knock at the bathroom door. "Bernie," came the plaintive wail, "what is a whisk?"

Please, keep it simple.

4. HAVE ENOUGH HELP
Yes, Lady Marjorie, you should have at least three in help: a chef, a butler, a maid. If you can handle all three jobs yourself, do so. If you can't, don't. If you need a week in the tropics to recuperate from a party, you don't have enough help.

5. DON'T WORRY ABOUT UNCLE GEORGE
Uncle George doesn't eat eggs, or anything made with wheat flour. He's allergic to smoke, to noise and probably to people. Do not in any circumstances plan your party around Uncle George. If he does have dietary restrictions and informs you of them *in time*, you might plan a special dish for him—an eggless, wheatless quiche, for example—or ask him to bring his own.

The same goes for the bar. Two days before a wedding reception planned for champagne and wine, the very nervous bride-to-be, a stewardess, called to say that she *had* to have a full bar because her Uncle George (yes, he has become a generic term for us) was coming, and *had* to have his Scotch. On the day of the wedding, the champagne and wine flowed as planned, and Uncle George was royally treated to as much Scotch as he wanted, served from the little liquor bottles they use on the airplanes. He felt special—if indeed he felt anything—and the tone of the party was not changed. Remember, when you plan a party, that you are not a restaurant.

6. GET KNOWN FOR A SPECIALTY
You may not have the beauty, charm and social cachet of a Jackie O. or the means of Midas, but, even so, your parties can be memor-

able. We know of one party giver who is famous for her asparagus. Every year she gives an asparagus buffet that celebrates spring. Nor are there ever any squawks amid the stalks. It helps your party-giving image if you develop a specialty—in food, in décor, in the mix of your guests. One of our specialties is chocolate. Martin has even been dubbed "the Chocolate Chef," and we could hardly do a party without a chocolate dessert. Needless to say, several of the desserts in this book are tall, dark and handsome.

7. NEVER APOLOGIZE

Don't be negative. Don't point out the cracks in the ceiling that only *you* know are there. Don't apologize for the food. Serve the fallen soufflé as your *special* fallen soufflé.

8. INVOLVE YOUR GUESTS

Kids' parties are fun because everyone participates. Remember the child in each of your guests and get them all to participate. Invite early comers into the kitchen to help with your final preparations. Or put them to work at the bar. Serve food that invites participation—a gazpacho with an assortment of garnishes to choose from becomes a kind of make-your-own-sundae soup. Above all, remember that people come to parties mainly to have fun.

9. FORGET ALL THE OTHER RULES AND DO IT YOUR WAY

Your party should be a statement of your personal tastes, preferences, fancies. Give the party that makes *you* comfortable, and you will have a successful party.

10. SMILE

Your guests will take their cues from you.

How to Plan a Party

There are three interdependent factors to consider in the conception of a party: the occasion, the budget, and the type of party. As in the case of the chicken or the egg, it doesn't matter which factor comes first when you hatch the idea, but it is important that all three come into consideration during the incubation process. That way, you'll never lay an egg.

THE OCCASION

You know a good deal more about why you are giving a party than we do, so we will simply encourage you with an aphorism:

• Celebrate every special occasion with a party; make every party a special occasion.

THE BUDGET

Here, *we* can be of help if *you* can be honest. Determine what you would like the party to cost—either in total, or per person, whichever way is easiest for you to work out. Then make a list of estimated expenditures—for food, labor, bar and miscellany—for the type of party you are planning. If you have a relatively low budget in mind, then it's obvious that you can't produce an epic, so don't try. Do something modest, but well—a small brunch, for example. However, if you have a relatively high budget in mind, you might want to hire a good professional caterer; or fly in your own foie gras and truffles and skip the middleman. In any case, you must have a firm idea of your budget *before* you settle on the type of party.

THE TYPE OF PARTY

Obviously, some parties are less expensive than others—and a less expensive party will allow you to invite more guests. A Sunday brunch for 30 people may well cost less than a Saturday-night dinner for 20; a cocktail reception for 100 less than a buffet luncheon for 75.

If you are starting with a specific occasion—a wedding, for example—do not feel obliged to produce a certain type of party. There is no law that says wedding guests must be given a seated dinner. Determine, first, the number of guests you would like to invite, your budget, and the type of party that *you would really like to give.* (Beware of unsought advice in this: We have seen too many good party ideas turned into mutants by well-meaning friends and relatives eager to graft their ideas onto the host's.) If your idea of a lovely wedding party is a champagne and hors d'oeuvres reception in the garden, then do it, and tell Cousin Sarah to have *her* wedding banquet at Maison de la Flocked Wallpaper when her turn comes.

The Guest List and Invitations

Make up a guest list and send out invitations. The format of party invitations varies considerably—from the most formal hand calligraphy to the least formal telephone call. Whatever format you choose, remember to include:

• *who* is giving the party

- *what* kind of party
- *where* it will be given
- *when* it will be given
- *why*—if there is a special reason
- *request for a reply* to your invitation (RSVP and telephone number; if invitees do not respond, call them to find out if they are coming)

Be certain your invitations make clear what you will be serving your guests. This can be done in two ways: by the time you set for the party and by the name you give it. For example, *Cocktail Party, from 4-6 P.M.* tells guests they are not getting dinner; *Cocktail Buffet, from 5-8 P.M.* tells them they will be served more and heartier food, which they may make into dinner; *Surprise Omelette Supper, from 10 P.M.-?* tells guests even more—although if you put a question mark at the end of the time frame, you may have to yawn a lot at the end of the evening.

Planning the Menu

A good rule for any party is to offer food that your guests usually do not have at home. Party food should be different and, of course, absolutely excellent. One of our close friends and eating companions has lately given us a new short vocabulary with which to rate party dishes. "This is *good,*" Keith will say of a sauce Béarnaise, "good, but not *special,*" emphasizing the key word with a finger jab and often a repeat. "But

this chocolate torte," he will exclaim, eyes sparkling in absolute abandon, "is *special, really special.*"

That's the way your guests should feel about the food at your party; it must be *special, really special.* But let us hasten to add that "special" and "different" do not mean exotic. Pâté of eel may have its place among the food faddies of the world, but the food at your party should be adventurous without being pretentious. Know your guests, and cook to their tastes.

There has to be a practical as well as an aesthetic side to planning the menu for a party. Make sure that you have the time, skill and ability to prepare the food you plan. Make sure you have the pans to cook it in and the bowls to serve it in. Select recipes that can be made ahead, in whole or in part, and foods which can be served at room temperature as well as those which must be served steaming hot.

In planning a party menu, consider all of the nutritional factors that would pertain in the planning of any well-balanced meal.

And, of course, consider cost.

The Bar

There are books that will tell you how to set up a liquor bar for a party: so-and-so many bottles of such-and-such, based on national averages as mysteriously arrived at as TV ratings. We don't think much of these. Tastes vary so much from place to place and from one social set to another that your best bet is a quiet consultation with the man at your local liquor store. From his perspective he can probably give you much better estimates of how much of what to buy than you would ever get from any national averages. (It may also be possible to arrange for the return of any unopened bottles; do ask.)

Our philosophy of party drinks often precludes any necessity for a full liquor bar. We think parties should feature drinks that have all the aesthetic appeal of party food: different, special and not exotic. Pass trays of champagne and Kir Royale (page 75) at a wedding reception and create a distinctive ambiance. Run an open bar, and you're mimicking the tavern down the street.

At parties, we prefer wine—both red and white—to hard liquor because it complements the taste of food instead of obliterating it. And in agreement with Alec Waugh, we prefer champagne to almost anything except a good red burgundy. However, if you and your guests prefer hard liquor to all else, disregard our argument and by all means do it your way. But again, make it special. Buy the 12-year-old Scotch that you have been intending to try, and share it with your guests, who have been meaning to try it too.

Setting up a bar for a party involves much more than the selection of wine and liquor. You must have appropriate glassware, soft drinks, ice. You must decide where and how to serve what. You must have someone to pour and serve—and someone to wash the glasses. We use

the checklist below to make sure everything is taken care of—and you may want to adapt it for your own needs.

```
┌─────────────────────────────────────────────┐
│              BAR CHECKLIST                   │
│                                              │
│ URGENT                               DONE    │
│ ☐  1. Wine:_____ ☐        │
│ ☐  2. Liquor:_____ ☐        │
│ ☐  3. Glassware:_____ ☐        │
│ ☐  4. Ice:_____ ☐        │
│ ☐  5. Sodas:_____ ☐        │
│ ☐  6. Juices:_____ ☐        │
│ ☐  7. Garnishes:_____ ☐        │
│ ☐  8. Water Pitcher:_____ ☐        │
│ ☐  9. Cocktail Napkins:_____ ☐        │
│ ☐ 10. Bar Cloths:_____ ☐        │
│ ☐ 11. Wine Bucket:_____ ☐        │
│ ☐ 12. Ice Bucket:_____ ☐        │
│ ☐ 13. Trays:_____ ☐        │
│ ☐ 14. Other:_____ ☐        │
│ ☐ 15. Special Instructions:_____ ☐        │
│ ☐ 16._____ ☐         │
│ ☐ 17._____ ☐         │
│ ☐ 18._____ ☐         │
│ ☐ 19._____ ☐         │
│ ☐ 20._____ ☐         │
│    NOTES                                     │
│                                              │
│ Function:_____  No. of Bars:_____    │
│ No. of Guests:_____  Location:_____    │
│ Time of Arrival:____  _____     │
│                       _____     │
│ Bartenders:_____   │
└─────────────────────────────────────────────┘
```

GLASSWARE

Except for the most casual picnic or boat party, plastic cups are out (use them only when you use paper plates). But you needn't go to the other extreme and provide *the* correct glass for each beverage, unless you are serving dinner to the Wine and Food Society. For a majority of parties we recommend a single type of glass—an all-purpose balloon wine goblet with a capacity of about 12 ounces. Filled halfway, it's fine for wine and champagne; for soft and hard drinks over ice, you can fill it to the brim. It is also suitable for water during dinner, and for Cognac afterwards.

ICE

Even if you have the newest, most efficient ice-spewing mechanism known to the modern refrigerator-freezer, we still recommend buying ice for your party. The ice prepared in your home freezer may easily pick up odors from the wonderfully aromatic party food stored in your refrigerator. It may also take you an entire day to prepare enough ice for your party. Commercially prepared ice cubes are generally crystal-clear, odor-free and a small investment for a good drink. You might also want to buy enough ice to chill the wine and champagne. (Chill the bottles in a wash tub or utility sink.) It usually takes less than an hour on ice to chill wine and champagne, while it can take all day—and all of the space—in your refrigerator.

SOFT DRINKS

Here again, the selection of nonalcoholic and carbonated beverages will be determined by your taste and those of your guests; but it is generally a good idea to have on hand cola, diet cola, sparkling water, and perhaps ginger ale or a lemon-flavored soft drink. If you plan an open bar, you will also need tonic water. If you really prefer not to serve soft drinks, but feel you must have them, store them out of sight under the bar, and serve them only when a guest specifically asks for them.

LOGISTICS

Where and how you set up your bar will depend on the type of party, the drinks you plan to offer, and the number of people you plan to serve. For small, informal parties you may want to have the bar set up in the kitchen; for the more formal evenings, on a sideboard—or, if you have one, at your bar. For larger parties, we suggest you have several bar stations—perhaps a self-service wine bar and a whatever-else-you-are-serving second bar. (Or you may have identical twins.) For large parties, where you want to avoid swarms of bar-flies at all costs, we strongly recommend that you also have waiters passing trays of drinks. It is elegant and most efficient.

Party Help

BAR HELP: A good professional bartender can serve 50 people at a cocktail party or buffet unless he has to blend Shirley Temples and frozen Daiquiris in addition to everything else. An inexperienced bartender can serve no one properly. For parties of 50 or more, you should have at least one more person, to pass drinks and to pick up used glasses (on a tray, please; not with the finger-in-the-glass method).

SERVICE STAFF: In many cities there are professional services which provide part-time party help. Many colleges and universities also have student bartender and waiter services. When hiring party staff, determine ahead of time:
- *manner of dress*—ask how the staff is usually uniformed and indicate any special requests you may have.
- *pay schedule and work schedule*—these vary considerably from location to location, so make certain you establish ahead of time the fee to be paid and the number of hours to be worked. At what point will overtime commence? (Our professional party people usually work a five-hour shift—approximately an hour to set up, three hours for the party, and one hour for cleanup—and are paid a set fee for five hours. After that, they go on an hourly overtime rate.) Agency fees generally do not include gratuity, and you should always tip at least 15 percent.
- *duties and responsibilities*—make certain that you and the party employee understand exactly what is to be done.

agree that music at a formal dinner party can be an intrusion. On the other hand, there is nothing more romantic at a cocktail party than telling Sam to play it again. Background music can often make a party sound as if it is having a good time.

Some musical notes:

• Background music should remain in the background, both in the volume level and in the selection of music.

• If you plan to use music on tape or record, set up everything ahead and assign someone else the D.J. responsibilities. Don't fiddle with tapes all night—harmonize with your guests instead.

• If you are using live music for background (e.g., a cocktail piano or chamber ensemble), don't use amplifiers.

• When hiring professional or student musicians, refer back to the considerations for hiring party help on page 14. Don't hire musicians unless you have heard them play.

• The ideal way to present dance music is in its own space—a separate room (or tent). That way, those who want to dance can dance, and those who want to talk can talk.

The Ambiance

In the film "Father of the Bride" a family giving a too-large wedding in their too-small home remove all the furniture to a moving van for the day. Nowadays, they might well leave the furniture in place and have the party in the van.

Adapting your home for a large party, establishing circulation patterns, and so on are covered in detail on page 58. Remember, though, that in the time between now and your next party, you cannot turn your home into the Hall of Mirrors at Versailles. Don't try.

But do try a little artifice. For evening parties, dim the lights; replace reading bulbs with soft pink ones; candlelight your rooms, whenever possible, for sparkle.

Whatever the time of day, decorate with flowers. Create diversionary points of interest.

• *experience*—insist on an experienced person, not a novice.

• *exact specifications*—establish (and have the person who takes your order repeat in every detail) every specific about the job assignment: the date of party, time of staff arrival, your name, location and telephone number. (The best bartender in the world will not be much help if he shows up on the wrong night!)

Music at a Party

Music at a party, said one wag, is the last refuge of the insecure hostess. We are not certain that we can hum along with *that* tune, although we do

Treat your home as a stage set and banish anything inappropriate to the wings.

Keep table coverings and decorations simple. Unless you are a professional, draping your table with designer bedsheets will have a startling effect—it will look exactly like a table covered with bedsheets. Do not rummage through grandmother's attic for exotic rusticana to use as serving pieces, though fine old serving platters or baskets can sometimes be charming.

When you pick flowers for the party, consider the sensitive palate as well as the artistic eye. Never select strongly scented flowers for the table (nor strongly scented candles). We personally prefer that you don't use potted plants near food. If you are decorating with food, keep it simple. Don't bury tables under a "natural" landscaping of crudités and dips. We believe in kale, but not when the table needs a pruning.

Above all, do not overdo. Remember that elegance is born of simplicity.

* * * *

This book embodies our suggestions for entertaining different numbers of people, from 12 to 100, on five occasions: a formal dinner, a sequential buffet, a brunch, a big holiday buffet, and a cocktail party. There are five specific menus, but many of the recipes are interchangeable and we have tried to suggest alternatives, wherever possible. Good recipes for cooking in quantity are hard to find, and the book's primary purpose is to give you ideas and advice, based on our own experience. When all is said and done, however, the party that best suits your home and your personal style of living in it will be the most successful—because it truly reflects *you*.

A PARTY PLANNING GUIDE

Below is an adaptation of a planning guide we use for parties, which coordinates the menu, timetable for cooking, garnish and plating, special equipment—and even a shopping list. Use this form or create your own, but please, do it!
(In addition to this chart, you should have three others: a bar checklist (page 13), a list of rental equipment (see page 19), and, of course, your guest list.)

DATE: _____ OCCASION: _____ NO. OF GUESTS: _____ TIME: _____

STAFF: _____ REMINDERS: _____

Timetable	Menu Item	Quantity	Ingredients	Garnish & Plating	Special Equipment

Party Rentals

Only you and your investment banker know for certain if you have enough china, glassware, silverware and linens to meet your party needs; but if you are like most of us, you may very well have to rent equipment. There is a vast assortment available to you, everything from coat racks and chafing dishes to lecterns for your next Academy Awards acceptance speech.

What to Rent

After you have planned your bar and menu, ask your local party rental company to provide you with a list of items available for rent. Having this list in front of you will help to organize your thoughts, and remind you of items you might otherwise forget, or that you might not even know are rentable. The party rental people will also be able to help you put your order together.

Quantities

Again, the rental company should advise you on how much equipment to order, but as an additional guide we have included a sample rental list for a cocktail reception (see opposite page). When ordering barware, keep in mind our recommendation to use an all-purpose wineglass and the checklist of bar equipment (page 13).

Quality

Most party rental services have showrooms. It is a good idea, especially if you are inexperienced, to preview exactly what you are renting. If there are several rental companies in your area, visit more than one. You will find a broad range of design, quality and cost of rental. Shopping around will save you money.

Seeing the equipment in person will probably save you money in another way. You will note that the less expensive stainless steel forks for rent are exact replicas of the silver ones, and are quite suitable for your buffet; that the machine-made wineglasses, although not hand-blown, are fine; that the glass ashtrays and salt and pepper shakers will look better with your decor than the silver ones that are three times as costly.

When placing your order, stress that you expect good equipment in good shape. You want this year's models, you want them in perfect condition, and you want them clean. This is important! (Some companies have a surcharge for new or "deluxe" equipment, and in some cases it is advisable to pay more to avoid getting casualties of the rental wars.)

Procedure

Place your rental order as early as you can, to guarantee getting what you want. (Just try, for example, to rent red tablecloths, "deluxe" or otherwise, the week before Christmas!) You can, and usually will, adjust the order several days before the party, adding items that you forgot, correcting the number of glasses, setting up the delivery schedule, etc.

Usually rental companies deliver everything the day before the party, a good idea because it leaves margin for error. Upon delivery, take the time to examine and count everything carefully. Once you accept the order, you are responsible for it. When unpacking the items, pay attention to how they are packed, as you will be expected to repack them after the party.

Generally, you do not have to put rented glassware, crockery and cutlery through the washer (everything will be washed by the company upon its return), but you *are* required to rinse them off before repacking. For a large party, this usually means having someone at the sink throughout the party, rinsing and putting things away, or washing them for reuse if you are running short. So plan accordingly.

Pickup of rental items is usually arranged for the day after the party. Again, you should take inventory, because you will be held responsible for loss or breakage—which is only fair.

Instant Expertise

Make notations on your list of rental equipment as to whether you needed more glasses, fewer silver trays, etc., and save this annotated list for reference. The next time you place an order for party rentals, you will do so with the suave assurance of a banquet manager.

Sample Rental List: Gala Cocktail Buffet for 50

BAR
120 12-ounce all-purpose wineglasses
   (order at least 2 glasses per person)
2 ice tubs (to chill wine and champagne)
1 plastic runner (to protect floor behind bar)
2 ice buckets (display champagne in one; ice drinks from second)
2 bar pitchers
2 6-inch silver bowls (for bar garnishes)

ICE
2 40-pound bags (half to chill wine and champagne; half to serve with drinks)

TABLES
1 8-by-2½-foot table (to set up buffet)
1 6-by-2½-foot table (to set up bar)
4 24-inch round tables (cocktail tables for terrace)
12 white folding chairs (around cocktail tables)

CLOTHS
4 84-inch round pink tablecloths (for cocktail tables)
4 72-by-120-inch pink tablecloths (2 per large table)
4 matching napkins (for bartender)

(NOTE: all tablecloths draped to the floor.)

SERVING TRAYS
16 14-inch round silver trays (12 for plating food; 4 for passing)
1 large handled silver tray (for fillet of beef)

MISCELLANEOUS
1 large garbage can (kept in kitchen)
16 glass ashtrays (around apartment)
24 votive candles (around apartment)
1 coat rack (holds 40 coats; in fur coat season, order 2 racks)

A Menu for Dinner for 12:
The Fête Accompli

HORS D'OEUVRES

French Farmhouse Pâté

Cornichons • Dijon Mustard • French Bread

FIRST COURSE

*Gazpacho with Garlic Croutons or *Artichoke Vinaigrette*

MAIN COURSE

Breast of Chicken Baked with Onions, Cheeses and White Wine
Herbed Rice • *Sautéed Snow Peas and Carrot*

DESSERT

*Chocolate "Fettucini" with Chantilly Cream
and Dark Chocolate Sauce*

BEVERAGES

Champagne • White Wine
Coffee • Tea • Espresso

*In each of the five menus in this book,
asterisks indicate that recipes for suggested
dishes are included in the section that follows.
Page references are given when recipes appear in
other sections. The remaining items are suggested
accompaniments to round out each menu.*

The challenge when having friends in for dinner is to serve a delicious and (let's face it) impressive meal without being frazzled, harried or out of sight in the kitchen. Your friends come to sip and to sup and to *see you*, so you have two choices:

1. Bring them into the kitchen for a kitchen party—which is fine if you have a large enough kitchen (and according to the food magazines, doesn't everyone?), and if you have the assurance to prepare a meal for 12 in plain view; or,

2. Plan a menu that can be assembled and served without your disappearing for long stretches of time. We suggest the latter course of action, which is much safer. Watching a chef flambé in his television kitchen is fun, but singeing your own eyebrows in front of company is definitely not.

One key to a menu that won't require your ongoing attention in the kitchen is to serve as many cold or room-temperature courses as you can. The hors d'oeuvres (if any), can certainly be cold. So can the first course, salad (if any) and dessert. That leaves only one course to be presented hot and with appropriate flourish, and even this one course should be designed for ease of preparation and service.

The menu we recommend satisfies all these requirements. The hors d'oeuvres, first course and dessert are all made ahead and served cold. The main course is an assemblage, all of whose components can be prepared ahead. They are then layered and baked to a turn while you are chatting with your guests. We also present a method for preparing rice ahead and keeping it at ideal serving condition. Only the vegetable—a quick sauté of snow peas and carrot—requires actual cooking just before serving. (You can, of course, substitute any vegetable in season.)

The dessert is designed to be fun: a large bowl of "pasta" which you toss at the table with cream, and top with a rich chocolate sauce. This is a new creation of ours and, we hope, a new sensation of yours.

NOTE: Gazpacho is served mostly in warm weather because people like to eat cold soups when it's hot (and also winter tomatoes tend to taste like cardboard). An alternative first course is Artichokes Vinaigrette, a simple and elegant way to start any meal.

French Farmhouse Pâté

Makes 1¾ pounds

Everyone has a favorite coarsely textured country French pâté. This is ours, and it is often the hit of the party. If you can't find unsalted pistachio nuts, hazelnuts work nearly as well.

We use clarified butter in this and several other recipes because it does not burn as readily whole butter. Simply melt the butter and skim off the white foam. Pour off the clear golden liquid (clarified butter), discarding the milky residue at the bottom of the pan. Prepare it in quantity and store in the refrigerator for use as needed.

½ pound thinly sliced bacon
2 tablespoons clarified butter
6 ounces calves' liver, in ½-inch slices
1 medium-size onion, finely chopped
2 large cloves garlic, finely chopped
⅓ cup Cognac
1 large egg, lightly beaten
½ pound ground veal
½ pound ground fatty pork
¼ pound thickly sliced double-smoked bacon, cut into ¼-inch dice
½ teaspoon salt
½ teaspoon freshly ground pepper
½ teaspoon dried thyme or 1 tablespoon fresh thyme, finely chopped to release the flavor
¼ cup unsalted shelled pistachio nuts, cut in half
Optional garnish: tomato rose, cornichon "fans," parsley sprigs

Preheat the oven to 350 degrees.

Line a 1-quart crock with the thinly sliced bacon, overlapping the slices slightly and extending the ends several inches over the rim of the crock.

Heat the clarified butter in a sauté pan over high heat, and when hot, quickly sear the liver on both sides. Remove from the pan and set aside.

Reduce the heat to moderate and cook the onion until translucent. Add the garlic and cook for about a minute more. Add the Cognac and flambé. When the flames die, transfer the onion mixture to a large mixing bowl. Cut the liver into ½-inch cubes and add it to the onions. Add all the remaining ingredients and mix well. Spoon the mixture into the crock, and fold the bacon back to cover the pâté. Seal it tightly with foil and place on a baking sheet. Bake in the middle of the oven for 1 hour. Then remove the foil and bake for another 20 minutes until the pâté juices run yellow, not pink, and its internal temperature reaches 140 degrees or more on a meat thermometer.

Remove the pâté on its baking sheet from the oven. Allow to cool for about 20 minutes, then carefully pour off most of the juices. Cover loosely with foil, and place a 2-pound weight on top. When the pâté has cooled, remove the weight, cover tightly with foil and refrigerate. Allow the flavors to develop for at least 1 day before serving.

To serve, unmold the pâté (run a knife around the edge, or dip the crock briefly into warm water). Cut it in half and place half on a serving platter for display, garnished with a tomato rose, parsley and cornichon fans. Slice the remainder and serve with more cornichons, Dijon mustard and rounds of freshly sliced French bread.

NOTE: To make the unmolding process easier, before filling the crock, cut an 8-inch piece of foil, fold it into a 2-inch-wide strip, and place at the bottom of the crock with its ends extending up over the sides. Pull up on the ends of the strip to loosen the chilled pâté.

Gazpacho with Garlic Croutons

Serves 12-14

This version of Gazpacho, with its colorful assortment of garnishes, is fun at a party, and there is no need to serve a salad—because your guests are eating their salad with a spoon. Puree the soup in the food processor; but dice all the vegetables by hand, because no processor does the job as evenly. Do not make the gazpacho too far ahead, or it will lose its fresh flavor and become too garlicky.

9-10 medium-size tomatoes, peeled, seeded and diced
1 medium-size onion, diced
2 cucumbers, peeled, seeded and chopped
2 green peppers, seeds and ribs removed, finely chopped
2 cloves garlic, chopped
3-4 scallions, white and green parts, thinly sliced
3 cups canned tomato juice
6 tablespoons olive oil
6 tablespoons red wine vinegar
2 teaspoons salt, or to taste
Freshly ground black pepper, to taste
Tabasco sauce, to taste
3 cups Garlic Croutons (see below)

Place 3 cups diced tomato, the diced onion, ¾ cup diced cucumber, ¾ cup green peppers and the chopped garlic in a large mixing bowl. Stir to combine. Refrigerate the remaining diced vegetables and the sliced scallions in separate covered containers to be used as garnishes.

Process about a third of the mixed vegetables in a food processor fitted with a steel blade to make a smooth puree. Add 1 cup tomato juice, 2 tablespoons olive oil and 2 tablespoons red wine vinegar. Process until smooth and well blended. Transfer to a large bowl. Repeat this procedure twice more, until you have pureed all of the vegetable mixture with the tomato juice, oil and vinegar. Stir the pureed soup thoroughly and season to taste with salt, pepper and Tabasco. Cover and chill for at least 2 hours.

Before serving, use a slotted spoon to transfer each of the vegetable garnishes to individual small serving bowls. Put the garlic croutons in larger bowls. Stir the soup well and adjust the seasoning. Serve ice cold with the bowls of garnishes attractively arranged on a tray. Place a demitasse spoon in each bowl so guests can help themselves.

GARLIC CROUTONS

Makes 3 cups

2 cloves garlic
6 tablespoons olive oil
3 cups cubed Italian or French bread, cut in ½-inch cubes

Preheat the oven to 325 degrees.

Lightly smash the garlic cloves with the flat heel of a chef's knife. Remove the skin and discard. Place the garlic in the oil to macerate. Arrange the bread cubes on a baking sheet in a single layer, and place in the oven for about ½ hour until dry and hard.

Reserve 2 tablespoons of the oil and pour the rest, with the garlic, into a heavy-bottomed sauté pan. Heat over high heat until bubbles appear around the garlic. Reduce the heat and fry the garlic, turning it constantly with a slotted spoon, until light brown. Discard it, increase the heat, and add the bread cubes. Fry, tossing frequently, until golden brown. Add the reserved oil, as needed. Remove the croutons, cool to room temperature, and serve.

Artichoke Vinaigrette

Some of the most elegant restaurants in the world serve artichokes as a first course. You may wish to try one of the more interesting presentations, such as painstakingly removing the cooked leaves and arranging them on a plate in overlapping concentric circles with the heart at the center. The heart may be filled with dressing, caviar or attractive vegetable garnishes. However, for practicality, we suggest you serve the artichokes whole, one to each guest, accompanied by the dressing in an individual dish or bowl.

12 medium-size artichokes
1 lemon, cut in half
2 teaspoons salt
3 cups Creamy Vinaigrette Dressing
(recipe follows)

Bring 2 large pots of water to a rolling boil over high heat (or use 1 large pot and cook 6 artichokes at a time). Cut off the stem end of each artichoke flush with the bottom (allowing it to stand upright). Remove and discard the tough outer bottom leaves. Cut off the sharp pointed tip of each leaf with stainless steel scissors. Rub all of the cut surfaces with the half lemon as you go to prevent discoloration.

Add the salt to the rapidly boiling water and stir. Carefully lower 6 artichokes into each pot and return to the boil. Reduce the heat and simmer until the artichokes are tender. Test by inserting the tip of a knife into the stem ends; it should enter easily.

Remove the artichokes with a slotted spoon and turn them upside down to drain. Allow to cool slightly. Using your fingers, gently separate the center leaves, reach in and carefully pull out the sharp pointed leaves from the center. Remove the choke (the hairlike fibers which cover the heart), with a teaspoon—but be sure not to remove any of the delicious heart. Serve the artichokes warm or at room temperature, but *do not refrigerate* them. That will change their taste and texture.

NOTE: One of the secrets of cooking vegetables so that they retain their color and flavor is to use an abundance of rapidly boiling water. Ideally, when you immerse vegetables in the water, they should begin to cook immediately, and a low boil should be maintained throughout.

Creamy Vinaigrette Dressing with Tarragon and Parsley

Makes about 3 cups

The vinaigrette to serve with artichokes must be flavorful but delicate. This recipe satisfies that requirement. Lots of chopped parsley adds texture (one could almost call it meatiness) to the dressing.

⅔ cup tarragon vinegar (white wine vinegar flavored with tarragon)
1 cup olive oil
1 cup vegetable oil
1-2 cloves garlic, chopped
5 teaspoons Dijon mustard
1 tablespoon dried tarragon, preferably French
2 egg yolks
½ teaspoon salt, or to taste
¼ teaspoon freshly ground black pepper, or to taste
6 drops Tabasco sauce, or to taste
½ cup chopped parsley

Place all the ingredients, except the parsley, in the bowl of a blender. Process at high speed until well blended. The flavors will develop in about 1 hour. Stir in the chopped parsley and serve.

To serve with artichokes, spoon a tablespoon or two of the dressing into the center cavity of each artichoke. Also serve a side dish of sauce for each guest.

Breast of Chicken, Baked with Onions, Cheeses and White Wine

Serves 12

This is a rich and aromatic dish for a dinner party and quite easy. If you prepare the onions and the cheese-crumb mixture in advance, you need only trim the chicken breasts and assemble the dish on the day of the party. Putting it all together takes no more than 5 minutes, and as the dish bakes, it makes its own wonderful sauce. Use only the best cheeses and a good dry white wine.

4 large onions, thinly sliced (about 1 pound)
12 tablespoons unsalted butter
½ pound (about 2 cups) grated imported Reggiano Parmesan cheese (use medium-sized side on hand grater)
½ pound (about 2 cups) shredded Swiss Gruyère cheese (shred by hand)

Cook the onions in 4 tablespoons butter in a covered saucepan over moderate heat until soft and translucent (about 15 minutes). Do not let them brown. (If you are preparing the onions ahead, cook them and then refrigerate them in a covered container.) Mix the 2 cheeses with the paprika and breadcrumbs. (Refrigerate this mixture, too, in a covered container if preparing ahead.) Cut the 6 chicken breasts in half to make 12 portions in all, and remove all the skin, fat, tendons and membranes.

When ready to assemble and bake: Preheat the oven to 325

2 teaspoons sweet Hungarian
  paprika
1 cup fine dry breadcrumbs
6 whole boneless chicken breasts
  (about 8-10 ounces each)
Salt, to taste
Freshly ground white pepper,
  to taste
1 cup dry white wine
1½ cups chicken stock, preferably
  homemade

degrees. Set a rack in the upper third of the oven. Coat the inside of a baking dish or casserole (at least 2 inches deep and large enough to hold the breasts in a single layer) with 4 tablespoons butter. (If you like, you may use 2 baking dishes, each holding 6 breasts.)

Spread half of the onions in an even layer in the bottom of the dish. Salt and pepper both sides of the chicken breasts and arrange them, smooth side up, in an even layer over the onions. Spread the remaining onions evenly over the chicken. Sprinkle the cheese and crumb mixture evenly over the onions, covering the surface completely. Cut 4 tablespoons of the butter into ½-inch cubes and dot evenly over the crumbs.

Combine the white wine with the chicken stock, and carefully drizzle the mixture over the crumbs to moisten. Bake, uncovered, in the preheated oven for about 1 hour. The top should be nicely browned. Reduce the temperature to the lowest setting and let rest for about 15 to 30 minutes.

To serve, use a spatula to lift each serving from the baking pan, being careful not to disturb the browned top. Spoon the sauce next to the chicken (not over it), and place herbed rice over the sauce.

NOTE: This recipe can easily be halved or doubled. You can also substitute veal for the chicken when you feel extravagant. Have your butcher cut veal steaks from the leg, each about ½ inch thick and 4 to 5 ounces in weight. Bake for 1 hour and 15 minutes at 325 degrees, and let rest in the warm oven for another 15 minutes.

Herbed Rice

Serves 12-14

You really can prepare rice half an hour before serving and keep it warm over steam. The steaming actually improves the texture, separating the grains and making the rice fluffier.

5 quarts water (approximately)
1 tablespoon salt
3 cups long-grain Carolina rice
4 tablespoons unsalted butter, at
  room temperature
1 cup parsley, chopped
Freshly ground white pepper,
  to taste

Bring the water to a boil in an 8-quart saucepan. Add 1 tablespoon salt and stir. Slowly sprinkle the rice into the water, maintaining the boil. Stir once. Reduce the heat slightly, but keep the water at a low boil. Cook, uncovered, for about 14 minutes, periodically skimming off the foam that rises to the top and testing for doneness by tasting. Strain the rice through a large fine-mesh strainer held over the sink, and rinse, still in the strainer, under cold running water. Transfer the rice to the center of a large dampened kitchen towel and fold the edges up and over, making a bundle with the rice at the center.

Fill the saucepan with 2 inches of water and bring to a boil over high heat. Put the bundle of rice into the strainer and set it over the boiling water. Reduce the heat to the *barest* simmer. Place a sheet of foil over the top of the pan, making a seal, cover with the lid and steam the rice until ready to serve.

Just before serving, carefully unwrap the towel and place the rice in a large mixing bowl with the softened butter. Toss gently with a spoon to blend. Add the chopped parsley and season to taste with salt and white pepper. Serve at once.

Sautéed Snow Peas and Carrot

Owning a cooking school where French, Chinese, Japanese and American dishes all cross our table has enabled us to experience, at first bite, the cross-pollination of food cultures. Here snow peas make a startlingly beautiful, crisp and delicious accompaniment to a rich main course. The carrot is for color. Slice it by hand, as thinly as you dare.

1¼ pounds fresh snow peas
1 carrot, peeled and cut into
**   very thin 2-inch-long matchsticks**
2 tablespoons unsalted butter
Salt, to taste
White pepper, to taste

Bring a large pot of water to a rolling boil. Remove the "strings" from the snow peas by gently grasping the string at the stem end and pulling along the length of the pod. Cut out and discard a small notched "V" at one end of each snow pea with a small paring knife. (This is purely for decoration.) Rinse carefully.

Add a generous pinch of salt to the boiling water, stir and add the snow peas. Blanch for a short time—about 10 to 20 seconds—just until they lose their rawness. They should be bright green and crunchy. Remove them from the water with a slotted spoon and transfer to paper towels to drain. Use a sheet of cardboard to fan the snow peas until they cool. (Alternatively, you may plunge them into cold water to stop the cooking.)

Blanch the carrot matchsticks for 10 to 15 seconds. They should be bright orange and still crisp. Remove them from the water, drain on paper towels and fan to cool.

Heat 2 tablespoons butter in a 12-inch sauté pan until bubbling. Add the snow peas, tossing lightly with a spoon to coat with butter and heat through. Do not overcook. Add the carrots and toss to combine with the snow peas. Season with salt and pepper, and serve at once.

NOTE: For this fanning technique of cooling vegetables, we are indebted to our dear friend and resident teacher of Japanese cooking, Elizabeth Andoh. Fanning vegetables avoids waterlogging and doesn't wash away flavor. Thank you, Elizabeth, from two of your greatest fans.

Chocolate "Fettucini" with Chantilly Cream and Dark Chocolate Sauce

Serves 12

The first time we prepared this dessert for a party, one of the hosts' children (underfoot in the kitchen) was completely enthralled. "Chocolate pasghetti," he squealed in delight. "No," corrected his very proper nanny, "chocolate spaghetti... Spa-Geh-Tee." She didn't know her noodles. In this fool-the-eye dessert, delicate chocolate crêpes are sliced into "fettucini" (not spaghetti), tossed with lightly beaten whipped cream and topped with a dark, rich chocolate sauce. Toss the "fettucini" at the table for a memorable party dessert.

CHOCOLATE CRÊPES

Makes about 30 6-inch crêpes

6 large eggs
1⅓ cups half-and-half or light cream
1⅓ cups water
¼ cup sugar
¼ teaspoon salt
6 tablespoons clarified butter (see page 23), melted and cooled, plus a small amount to grease the crêpe pan
1¾ cups Wondra flour
¼ cup unsweetened Dutch-process cocoa

To make the crêpes, process all the ingredients in the bowl of a food processor or blender until smooth. Let rest for at least 20 minutes. Grease a 6-inch crêpe pan with a small amount of clarified butter. Heat the pan over medium-high heat until a drop of water sizzles upon contact. Pour ¼ cup batter into the pan, swirl quickly to cover the pan bottom and return the excess to the bowl. Cook on 1 side until the edges brown lightly. Flip and cook for 15 to 20 seconds. Repeat until all the batter is used. Let the crêpes cool. Cover if holding for later use, but do not refrigerate.

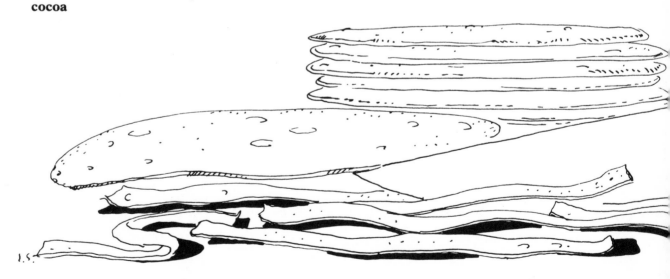

CHANTILLY CREAM

2 cups heavy cream,
  well chilled
2 tablespoons confectioners' sugar
2 teaspoons vanilla extract

To make the whipped cream, combine the ingredients and whip until soft peaks form. Cover and refrigerate.

DARK CHOCOLATE SAUCE

5 ounces semisweet chocolate,
  coarsely chopped
1 ounce unsweetened baking
  chocolate, coarsely chopped
½ cup brewed espresso coffee
¼ cup sugar
2 tablespoons almond-flavored
  liqueur
2 tablespoons unsalted butter

To make the chocolate sauce, melt all the chocolate in the top of a double boiler over hot (but not boiling) water. Dissolve the sugar in the hot espresso. Add this to the melted chocolate and blend well. Add the almond-flavored liqueur and butter. Blend well. Remove the sauce from the heat and cool. Reheat to warm before serving.

To assemble and serve: Cut each crêpe into long thin strands (about ⅜ inch in width) with a very sharp knife. Separate the strands carefully, toss them lightly with your fingers so that they resemble fettucini noodles and place them in a large shallow serving bowl. Gently form a well in the center and spoon the whipped cream into it. Pour the warm chocolate sauce into a sauce boat. Using 2 wooden spoons, toss the "fettucini" with the whipped cream to coat them. Serve in individual bowls, ladling warm chocolate sauce over each portion.

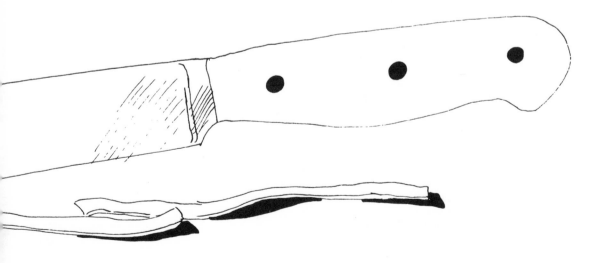

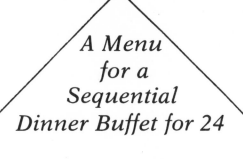

A Menu for a Sequential Dinner Buffet for 24

HORS D'OEUVRES

*Pâté of Chicken Livers with Cognac

*Sesame Melba Toast • *Crispy Glazed Cashews

FIRST COURSE

*Crabmeat Mousse with Green Goddess Sauce

MAIN COURSE

*Ragout of Veal with Fresh Mushrooms, Carrots and Onions • *Couscous

Small French Rolls • Salad of Mixed Greens, Vinaigrette (page 68)

DESSERTS

*Fresh Fruits in Champagne, or in *Grand Marnier Sauce

with Candied Orange Peel

or

*Compote of Dried Fruits with Almonds

BEVERAGES

Lillet on the Rocks with a Twist

White Wine • Red Wine

Champagne

Espresso

When we cater a dinner buffet in someone's home, we often suggest a very limited menu that closely resembles a sequential dinner. You needn't offer your guests an opulent array of highly stylized foodstuffs quivering under aspic, or chafing dishes gleaming all in a row like so many gold teeth. Let the grand hotels and luxury liners do that. Give your guests a good dinner—and a relaxed evening.

Put together a simple and elegant dinner menu:

FIRST SELECT THE MAIN COURSE
Revolutionary though this may sound, choose *one* entree. (If Uncle George wants *three*, send him on a cruise.) Consider stews (which sound much better if called ragouts) or braised dishes. These can usually be made ahead and reheated for the party. (During their day in the refrigerator, they are developing flavor while you are developing the rest of the party.) They also sit well in a chafing dish, an important consideration if you've ever watched beef go from hot pink to dull gray in minutes. Studding your stew with vegetables is even better—one less dish to cook and one less chafing dish to polish. Serve an interesting side dish that will sop up the sauce, such as noodles, rice or couscous, and you have a lovely, satisfying and *easy* main course.

CHOOSE A FIRST COURSE THAT GOES WELL WITH YOUR MAIN COURSE
Suppose you've followed sage advice and selected a ragout of veal with vegetables as your entree for dinner. You might then want a fish dish, something light and elegant, to start. Perhaps a Crabmeat Mousse with Green Goddess Sauce (page 37)? (Or scallops marinated in lime juice, or oysters on the half shell, or something with shrimp?)

So much for the First Course. Just make sure it has its own plate.

THE SALAD COURSE
Before you decide on a salad, decide where it goes. Will it share a plate comfortably with a hot ragout? Only if you arrange the noodles as a Maginot Line separating hot and cold. Does the salad rate a plate of its own? If you and your friends think so, then it does. How about a Spinach and Mushroom Salad (page 68), or a Mixed Green Salad with Julienne of Swiss Cheese and Endive (page 53), or a striking combination of arugula and red radicchio?

HORS D'OEUVRES
Do not overdo the overture or you will ruin the show. Guests must have something to eat during the cocktail "hour"—many people can't drink without eating. However, too many nibbles will definitely spoil dinner. A simple solution: Have some spreadables strategically placed, and instead of passing more hors d'oeuvres, *pass the first course*. Guests won't have to worry about ruining dinner because this will *be* dinner. Instead of a lot of inconsequential nibbles, they will have a real plate of food. For example, the crabmeat mousse you have decided upon can either be displayed on the buffet table alongside the main course and dessert, or it can be served on individual plates, passed to each guest. (If you think people can't handle a drink *and* a plate *and* a fork, just watch!)

DESSERT
One dessert or six? Serve one dessert at a buffet and you may lose friends; serve six and be called a temptress (or tempt*or*). Conclusion: Serve a couple of desserts *and* fresh fruit, or compotes made with fruit (see page 42). Most likely, even the diet-conscious sveltniks will take some of each, and come back for more. If possible, display the desserts during the party so people can gauge themselves accordingly.

Pâté of Chicken Livers with Cognac

Makes 6 cups

We always pack this pâté into shallow 2-cup plastic molds. This enables us to unmold and decorate one platter at a time, while keeping the remainder of the pâté refrigerated. The decorated platter is usually passed and then left at the bar or on a cocktail table. When its looks start to fade, we simply bring out a replacement. (Platters of food should never be left out during a party without being replenished or replaced.)

Make the pâté a day or two ahead to let the flavors develop. Serve it with Sesame Melba Toast (recipe follows) or crusty French bread, along with a butter knife for spreading.

**10 tablespoons butter,
  at room temperature**
**10 tablespoons chicken fat,
  at room temperature**
1⅓ cups chopped onions
**2 large cloves garlic,
  finely chopped**
2 pounds trimmed chicken livers
¾ cup chicken broth
1 teaspoon dried thyme, crushed
1½ teaspoons salt
**Freshly ground black pepper,
  to taste**
6 tablespoons Cognac
**4 hard-boiled eggs,
  coarsely chopped**
**Garnish: chopped parsley,
  tomato rose (optional)**

Heat 4 tablespoons butter and 4 tablespoons chicken fat in a 4-quart heavy-bottomed saucepan over moderate heat. Add the chopped onions and cook until soft and golden. Add the garlic and chicken livers, increase the heat and cook for another 2 minutes. Add the chicken broth, thyme, salt and pepper and continue to cook just until the livers are medium-rare (pink on the inside).

Transfer the livers and onions with a slotted spoon to a strainer over a bowl. Add to the pan any juices from the bowl and transfer the liver mixture from the strainer to the bowl. Bring the pan liquids to a boil and continue to boil until reduced to about 8 to 10 tablespoons. Add the Cognac, stir to blend and pour over the liver mixture. Cool.

Puree the cooled liver mixture in a food processor fitted with a steel blade. Add the chopped eggs and the remaining butter and chicken fat and continue processing until smooth. Adjust the seasoning. Line the mold (or molds) with plastic wrap. Spoon the pâté into the molds and tap them on the counter to eliminate air pockets. Cover and refrigerate for at least 4 hours.

To serve, unmold the pâté onto a serving platter, discard the plastic wrap and garnish with chopped parsley. If you like, decorate the top with a tomato rose.

NOTE: This recipe calls for 2 pounds *trimmed* chicken livers, which means that you must buy slightly more than this amount. Trim them well and discard any you don't feel completely positive about.

Sesame Melba Toast

Makes about 90 1-inch-wide strips

An untraditional melba toast that can be cut into strips, squares or triangles. We recommend strips for meat pâté and triangles for liver pâté or caviar.

**1 pound white bread, very
   thinly sliced**
**8 tablespoons unsalted butter,
   at room temperature**
¼ cup sesame seeds

Preheat the oven to 300 degrees.

Spread each slice of bread with a thin layer of butter. Cut off the crusts. Sprinkle the sesame seeds over the bread slices. Using the heel of the loaf, press the seeds gently into the butter. Cut each slice into 3 equal strips and place on a baking sheet. Bake on the center rack of the oven until golden brown. Cool and serve at room temperature.

NOTE: The melba toast can be stored in a covered container in the refrigerator for up to 2 weeks. Reheat in a 250-degree oven before serving.

Crispy Glazed Cashews

Makes 1 pound

These sweet and crispy cashews, a variation of a Chinese recipe, are a delightful surprise to serve with cocktails. Pecans or walnuts can be substituted for the cashews, if you prefer.

**1 pound unsalted cashew nuts (or
   salted cashews with the salt
   rinsed off)**
3 cups water
1 cup honey
12 tablespoons sugar
2 cups peanut or vegetable oil

Bring ½ pound cashews, 1½ cups water and ½ cup honey to a boil in a 2-quart heavy-bottomed saucepan. Boil for 5 minutes. Quickly drain the cashews, discarding the liquid, and return them to the pan. Place over moderate heat and add 6 tablespoons sugar. Remove from the heat and toss the cashews well in the sugar to coat them completely. Place the sugar-coated nuts in a single layer on wax paper (they should not touch each other) and let dry for at least 15 minutes. Wash the saucepan and repeat the procedure with the remaining half of all the ingredients (except the oil). Allow these nuts, too, to dry for at least 15 minutes.

Wash the pan and add the oil. Heat over medium-high heat until a cashew dropped into the pan begins to "bubble" almost instantly. Fry half the cashews, stirring constantly, until they are light brown and the sugar begins to caramelize. (Don't let them get completely brown or they will taste bitter.) Transfer, with a slotted spoon, to an absorbent kitchen towel to drain (they will stick to paper towel). Again, they must not touch each other. Fry the second batch of cashews, in the same manner, and drain.

When the nuts are completely cool and dry, they will be crisp. Use them at once, or store in an airtight jar for up to 1 week.

Crabmeat Mousse with Green Goddess Sauce

Serves 24

An elegant first course, particularly if you follow the presentation we recommend below. The tang of Green Goddess Sauce beautifully counterpoints the delicacy of the mousse. If prepared in an eight-cup fish mold, the mousse also makes a wonderful addition to the buffet table.

12 ounces fresh crabmeat, picked over carefully, or 2 5½- to 6½-ounce cans crabmeat, drained and liquid reserved
½-1 cup chicken broth
5 envelopes unflavored gelatin
¼ cup dry sherry
1 cup plus 2 tablespoons chopped onions
2 stalks celery, washed, peeled and chopped
½ cup parsley clusters
10 drops Tabasco sauce
½ teaspoon dried marjoram
6 large eggs, separated and at room temperature
1 cup plus 2 tablespoons mayonnaise
2 cups heavy cream

If using canned crabmeat, mix the drained liquid with enough chicken broth to make 1 full cup liquid. If using fresh crabmeat, use 1 cup chicken broth. Heat this cup of liquid to a simmer. Process the gelatin, sherry and hot liquid in a food processor fitted with a steel blade until the gelatin is completely dissolved. Scrape down the sides of the bowl with a rubber spatula, as necessary. Cool slightly. Add the remaining ingredients (except the heavy cream and the egg whites) and process to blend, again scraping the sides of the bowl, as necessary. With the motor running, add the heavy cream through the feed tube in a slow, steady stream and process to blend. Transfer the mixture to a large bowl.

Beat the egg whites until stiff, but not dry. Whisk about a third of the whites into the crabmeat mixture to lighten and then carefully fold in the rest. Divide evenly among 24 3-ounce molds, or spoon into an 8-cup fish mold. Chill until firm. Unmold and serve with Green Goddess Sauce (see next page).

Green Goddess Sauce

Makes about 2 cups

2 anchovy fillets
1 clove garlic
1½ cups mayonnaise
4 scallions with tops, coarsely cut
½ cup parsley clusters
1 tablespoon fresh lemon juice
1 tablespoon tarragon vinegar
6 drops Tabasco sauce
½ cup sour cream

Drop the anchovy fillets and garlic through the feed tube of a food processor fitted with a steel blade. Process until chopped, using a spatula to scrape down the sides of the bowl, as necessary. Add the remaining ingredients, except the sour cream, and process until well blended. Add the sour cream and process to blend. Transfer to a bowl, cover and refrigerate until well chilled.

A SPECIAL PRESENTATION

We have developed a special presentation of this dish which we would like to share with you.

1 recipe Crabmeat Mousse
1 recipe Green Goddess Sauce
Non-stick vegetable spray, such as Pam
24 3-ounce plastic cups with fluted edges and lids (available at delicatessens and ice cream shops—or use 3.5-ounce cups, and don't fill entirely)
24 puff pastry crescents*
24 thin slices young or hothouse cucumber, skin scored
3 ounces fresh red salmon caviar
24 ½-inch sprigs fresh dill

*Some specialty bakeries sell puff pastry crescents *(fleurons)*, or you can cut out your own from sheets of puff pastry, which may also be purchased.

Spray the inside of each plastic mold lightly with vegetable spray. Divide the crabmeat mousse evenly among the cups, cover with lids and refrigerate until firm.

Bake the puff pastry crescents in a 450-degree oven until puffed and browned. Set aside to rewarm before serving.

Cut each slice of cucumber once from the center (as if beginning to slice a pie), grasp each side of the cut with either hand and twist in opposite directions to make the slice resemble an "S."

To unmold the mousses, use scissors to cut a slit on either side of each mold. Jiggle the mold to release the mousse onto the center of a plate. Spoon 1 to 2 teaspoons of Green Goddess Sauce on the flat top of the mousse. (It should not run down the sides.) Top with 4 or 5 grains of caviar at the center and a dill sprig. Place an S-shaped cucumber slice at one side of the mousse and fit a warm pastry crescent to curve around the other side. Serve at once.

Another, easier garnish is to cut paper-thin slices of fresh lemon, lime or cucumber in half and arrange them decoratively around the rim of the dish.

Couscous

Couscous, precooked wheat semolina, is the traditional dish of Morocco, Algeria and Tunisia. It is becoming increasingly popular in the United States, because it is an incredibly light, delicate and unusual substitute for rice or noodles. (You should be able to find couscous in 16-ounce boxes at gourmet stores, and even in supermarkets, but you can also order it by mail.)*

Couscous is so easy to prepare that it almost makes up for the amount of time you spend preparing the ragout of veal. The mixture of parsley, lemon and garlic which is sprinkled over the top is decidedly not Moroccan, Algerian or Tunisian. You'll have to cross the Mediterranean to find its inspiration—the granolata of Italy.

3 16-ounce boxes couscous
7 cups chicken broth
 (approximately)
1 pound unsalted butter
 (approximately)
Garnish: ½ cup parsley-garlic-lemon
 mixture (see page 40)

Prepare the couscous according to the package directions, using the chicken broth and butter. (It will be easier if you prepare 1 box at a time; it only takes 3 to 4 minutes.) Fluff the couscous with a fork and combine. Steam over boiling water for about 15 to 20 minutes until light and fluffy.

To serve, place the couscous in a serving pan or bowl and sprinkle it with the reserved parsley mixture. It can be kept warm in a chafing dish over simmering water.

NOTE: Couscous can be prepared several days ahead, then covered and refrigerated. Reheat it in a steamer before serving. Couscous also reheats beautifully in a microwave oven.

*The Original Near East Couscous, Near East Food Products Inc., Leominster, MA 01453

Ragout of Veal with Fresh Mushrooms, Carrots and Onions

Serves 30

This ragout, redolent of citrus and tomato, should be made a day or two ahead, if possible, to let the flavors develop to the full.

Rind of 2 medium-size oranges
Rind and juice of 1 lemon
1 cup olive oil, more if needed
2 28-ounce cans Italian tomatoes,
    drained (3 cups juice reserved)
3 cups flour (more if needed),
    mixed with 1 tablespoon salt and
    2 teaspoons freshly ground
    black pepper
15 pounds boneless veal shoulder
    or neck, trimmed of fat or gristle
    and cut into 2-inch cubes
3 cups white wine
8-16 tablespoons clarified
    butter (see page 23)
2 cups finely chopped onions
2 cups finely chopped carrots
2 tablespoons finely chopped
    garlic
3 cups chicken broth
3-4 imported bay leaves
½ cup Cognac
½ cup finely chopped fresh basil
    (if not available, omit; do not
    use dried)
8 dozen fresh baby carrots (or
    8 dozen 2-inch pieces of larger
    carrots), peeled
8 dozen small white onions,
    peeled
8 dozen large mushroom caps,
    cleaned
Salt and freshly ground pepper,
    to taste
Garnish (and flavoring):
    Rind of 1 lemon, grated
    2 cloves garlic, finely chopped
    2 cups finely chopped parsley

Simmer the lemon and orange rinds in water to cover for 20 minutes. Drain and cut them into julienne strips. (Reserve the lemon juice for the mushrooms.) Put the tomatoes through a food mill or a strainer, and reserve the pulp.

Heat 3 to 4 tablespoons olive oil in a 12-inch heavy-bottomed sauté pan over high heat. Working in batches small enough to fit in the pan uncrowded, dredge the veal cubes lightly in the seasoned flour, shaking off the excess. Quickly sear the veal, turning the cubes to brown all sides. Transfer the browned meat to a large Dutch oven. Continue dredging and browning the veal in batches, adding more oil to the pan, as needed.

After browning approximately 3 pounds of veal, deglaze the pan with about ½ cup of white wine, scraping free all clinging food particles. Add this deglazing liquid to the veal in the Dutch oven. (Wash the pan if necessary.) Then add more oil to the pan and continue browning the veal in batches, deglazing the pan again after every 3 pounds of veal. When all the veal is browned, add any leftover wine to the Dutch oven and discard the unused flour.

Preheat the oven to 350 degrees.

Wash the sauté pan. Heat 2 tablespoons of the butter with 2 tablespoons olive oil in the pan over moderate heat. Add the chopped onion and carrot and cook until softened. Add the chopped garlic and cook for another minute. Transfer to the Dutch oven and add the stock, reserved 3 cups tomato juice, tomato pulp, julienned citrus rinds, bay leaves, Cognac and fresh basil. Bring to a boil over high heat, stirring occasionally. Cover the pot tightly and place it in the preheated oven for about 1½ hours, or until the meat is fork-tender.

While the veal is cooking, bring a large pot of water to a boil. Add a generous pinch of salt and then the carrots. Return to the boil, reduce the heat and simmer just until the carrots pierce easily with a knife. (Do not overcook.) Remove with a slotted spoon and fan to cool (see page 29) or plunge them in cold water. Set aside.

Discard the water and refill the pot. Bring the water to a

boil with a generous pinch of salt. Cut a small "X" at the root end of each onion and add to the water. Simmer the onions just until they pierce easily with a knife. (Do not overcook or they will fall apart.) Cool and set aside.

Leave the mushroom caps whole unless they are very large. Heat 4 tablespoons butter in the sauté pan over high heat and add mushrooms to fill the pan without crowding. Sprinkle on some lemon juice and cook on both sides until the mushrooms are just cooked through. Drain on paper towels. Repeat until all the mushrooms are cooked, using more butter and lemon juice as needed. Set aside.

When the veal is cooked, remove it from the sauce and set aside. Place the Dutch oven over high heat and reduce the sauce if it seems thin. Pass it through a food mill, and season to taste with salt and pepper.

If you are serving the ragout the same day, return the veal to the sauce and slowly bring to a boil, stirring. Add the vegetables and cook until heated through, stirring gently. Combine the grated lemon rind, chopped garlic and parsley. Fold two-thirds of this mixture into the ragout, reserving the rest to sprinkle on top (or over couscous; see recipe on page 39). Transfer the ragout to a chafing dish insert over simmering water. Garnish with the parsley mixture.

If you are making the ragout ahead, refrigerate the meat in its sauce, and each of the vegetables separately (or cook them the day of the party). To reheat, bring the meat and sauce slowly to a boil in the Dutch oven over moderate heat, stirring occasionally. When the meat is hot, add the vegetables, stirring gently, and cook until they are just warmed through. Make the parsley mixture, mixing two-thirds into the ragout and reserving the rest for garnish. Transfer the ragout to a chafing dish insert over simmering water and garnish with the parsley mixture.

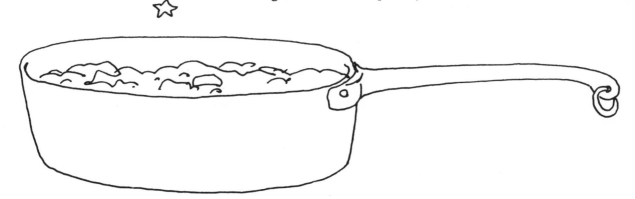

Fruit Desserts

Fruits are lovely after a party meal, and we like to offer them in the form of compotes, along with some special sauces. Choose combinations of fresh or dried fruit to complement the other dishes you are offering, both in color and taste. Take pains to prepare the fruit attractively (no pits, please), and vary the sauces to suit your fancy and the season.

Fresh Fruits in Champagne

Your choice of fruits
Superfine sugar, to taste
Champagne
Fresh mint, for decoration

Sweeten the fruit to taste with superfine sugar. Just before serving, moisten the fruit generously with champagne. Decorate with fresh mint and serve while the champagne is still bubbling. (You may substitute white wine for the champagne, but the effect will not be the same.)

Grand Marnier Sauce with Candied Orange Peel *Makes about 1 cup*

4 medium-size navel oranges
Water, as needed for preparing the peel
1½ cups sugar
2 tablespoons Grand Marnier

Using a vegetable peeler, remove the zest from the oranges in even strips about 1 inch by 3 inches. (Reserve the oranges to make orange segments for the fruit salad.) Using a sharp thin-bladed knife, cut the strips into very thin julienne (if you stack the strips, you can cut several at a time).

Place the strips in a saucepan with 3 cups water. Bring to a boil, reduce the heat and simmer for 5 minutes. Drain the strips and refresh in cold water. Repeat the process with 3 cups fresh water, simmering the strips for 5 more minutes. Again, drain and refresh in cold water, then drain again and pat dry with paper towels.

Combine the sugar and ½ cup water in a small heavy-bottomed saucepan. Bring to a boil and boil until the syrup reaches 230 degrees Fahrenheit on a candy thermometer. Remove from the heat, add the orange strips and let cool slightly. Add the Grand Marnier. Let the orange stripes macerate in the sugar syrup for at least 30 minutes before using.

NOTE: This sauce may be made weeks ahead and kept in the refrigerator. Rewarm it before using to dissolve any sugar crystals that may have formed.

Red Raspberry Sauce

Makes about 2 cups

A wonderful topping for Golden Rice Pudding (see page 69), fresh fruit, ice cream, et al. If you wish to make the sauce nonalcoholic, substitute orange juice for the Kirschwasser and add more sugar to taste.

4 10-ounce packages frozen raspberries, thawed, or 2 cups fresh raspberries
¼ cup Kirschwasser
½ cup superfine sugar, or to taste

Process the raspberries with their juices in a food processor fitted with the steel blade until pureed. Strain them into a bowl. Add the Kirschwasser and sugar, to taste. Stir to blend and serve chilled.

Compote of Dried Fruits with Almonds

Serves 24

Dried fruit desserts are much more popular in Europe than in this country, so we solicit your help in starting a new American trend. We find this dessert both simple and elegant.

4½ pounds assorted dried fruits (any combination, to taste, of prunes, pears, apricots, peaches, figs)
Water to cover
2½ cups sugar
2 2-inch cinnamon sticks
8 thin slices lemon
½ cup almond-flavored liqueur
2 cups blanched almonds, lightly toasted

Place the fruits in a large saucepan with water to cover, and bring to a boil. Add the sugar, cinnamon sticks and lemon slices. Reduce the heat and simmer, uncovered, for about 15 minutes or until the fruit is plumped and tender. Carefully remove the fruit from the saucepan, using a slotted spoon, and reserve. (If desired, discard the cinnamon sticks and lemon slices.)

Strain the syrup and return it to the pan. Raise the heat, bring to a rapid boil and continue to boil until the syrup thickens slightly. Remove the pan from the heat, stir in the liqueur and return the fruit (and any juices that have accumulated) to the pan. Allow to cool slightly.

Stir in the almonds, gently. Transfer the compote to a large serving bowl, or punch bowl. Serve warm or at room temperature.

NOTE: The compote may be made a day ahead and gently rewarmed to take off the chill. Do not add the almonds until *just* before serving. If you like, the compote may be accompanied by lightly whipped cream sweetened to taste with confectioners' sugar and vanilla.

A Menu for Brunch for 30: Omelettes or Crêpes Made to Order

BEVERAGES

*Bloody Marys with Horseradish or with Lime
Fresh Orange Juice • Champagne • White Wine
Coffee • Tea • Espresso

HORS D'OEUVRES

*Bacon-Wrapped Bananas, Prunes and Oysters
Prosciutto and Crunchy Asparagus, or Melon (page 82)

MAIN COURSE

*Omelettes (or *Crêpes) Made to Order, with a Choice of Fillings:
*Stir-Fried Oriental Vegetables • *Smoked Salmon in Cream Sauce with Dill
*Apple and Raisin Compote with Almonds

*Mixed Green Salad with Julienne of Swiss Cheese and Endive
Small Brioche or Croissant (served warm)
A Platter of Cheese and Fresh Fruit (page 83)

DESSERTS

*Pound Cake and Fresh Strawberries
with Chocolate Fondue
*Grapes Juanita

We assume that good fun is the object of your brunch, so if you don't mind showing off, we highly recommend omelettes *or* crêpes made to order for your guests. However, don't attempt to make omelettes *and* crêpes at the same party and don't attempt to make either until you have developed flawless technique. (If you don't feel like making either omelettes or crêpes, why not adapt items from the Holiday Buffet menu (page 56) to suit your needs?)

THE MENU: With omelettes or crêpes as the center of your menu, the time of day you choose for your brunch pretty much determines what else to serve. An early brunch, say ten-ish or eleven-ish (let's face it, that's the way people talk on Sunday morning), doesn't require much in the way of hors d'oeuvres. Just have the coffee ready (see page 71) and the omelette pans hot. On the other hand, a later brunch, starting after one in the afternoon, for example, may still be the first meal of the day for many guests, but it may also be their *only* meal of the day. Cook accordingly.

To plan the specifics of the brunch menu, first decide on either omelettes or crêpes. (To simplify things we'll choose omelettes for the duration of this discussion.) Then choose the fillings.

To us, the least imaginative type of omelette party is one in which the omeletteer confronts the omelettee with 42 little bowls of fillings. Often the resulting omelettes both look like and lead to indigestion. Also, by the time the omelettee makes up his/her mind, there is a waiting line of 12 hungry people, and an omeletteer with a smoking, overheated omelette pan. It is better to select several interesting omelette fillings. Take the time to prepare three fillings so tasty and unique that your omelettes qualify for the ultimate accolade: special, really special!

In this section, we present the recipes for three such fillings: one vegetable, one fish, and one fruit. Under no circumstances of taste or imagination can these three fillings be mixed together in one omelette—they are purposely mutually exclusive. Occasionally, guests may have two varieties of omelettes, or they may request that one of the other fillings be served as a side dish on their omelette plate. But each individual omelette stands alone—resplendent. This is good. Keep the rest of the meal simple: a crisp green salad, a warm baby brioche and a glass of chilled champagne. This is also good.

If you plan to serve hors d'oeuvres before the main course, remember that *brunch* is *breakfast* for many people. Serve canapes that feature breakfasty foods: smoked fishes, fruits, cheeses, bacon. Make certain that there is no duplication between the canapes and the omelette fillings— no stuffed mushrooms if you're serving mushroom omelettes, for example.

One technique we've discovered for coping with the inevitable line, albeit small, that forms at the omelette station is to have a cheese and fruit platter strategically placed within arm's reach of the line. People are not waiting for an omelette, you see, they're having cheese and fruit.

What about dessert for brunch? Since it's such an informal occasion, participation desserts always work well. Have a large basket of exquisite strawberries and cubes of homemade pound cake ready for your guests to dip into warm chocolate fondue. Or, if grapes are in season and you have spoons and bowls enough, offer Grapes Juanita, an almost instant dessert.

Bloody Marys for a Crowd

Makes 35 drinks

A Bloody Mary, the great American brunch drink, is simply flavored tomato juice spiked with vodka. To serve a crowd, prepare the tomato juice mixture ahead, transfer it to pitchers to pour at the bar, and stir in the vodka to order. Every bartender has a secret blend of flavorings; ours includes horseradish.

4 quarts tomato juice
1½ cups fresh lemon juice
½ cup prepared horseradish
Coarsely ground black pepper, to taste
Salt to taste
Worcestershire sauce, to taste
Tabasco sauce, to taste
4-5 lemons, cut into wedges, for garnish
1-2 ounces vodka per serving

Combine all the ingredients except the citrus wedges and vodka and stir to blend. Fill a 12-ounce all-purpose wineglass about halfway with ice cubes. Pour over ½ cup of the tomato juice mixture and add the vodka, to taste. Stir to blend and garnish with a lemon or lime wedge.

Variation: For Bloody Mary with Lime, substitute 1½ cups fresh lime juice for the lemon juice, a judicious quantity of celery salt for the horseradish, and use limes instead of lemons for garnish.

NOTE: For a very spicy New York-style Bloody Mary, we use about half a 5-ounce bottle of Worcestershire sauce and about 2 tablespoons Tabasco; we suggest you make a less spicy version and leave the hot sauce at the bar, so guests can add their own.

The Perfect Omelette

The technique for making omelettes is not difficult, but it must be learned, and once learned, *practiced*, particularly if you plan to show off in front of a crowd. If you are new at it, or want to build your confidence, we suggest that you buy two dozen eggs, clarify some butter and set to work. Make sure no one is watching, and prepare omelette after omelette until you perfect your technique. Discard your mistakes—feed them to the cat or chop them into Chinese fried rice. In any case, two dozen eggs is a small price to pay for almost-instant expertise, and look at the money you'll save by not hiring a caterer.

Here are some fail-safe tips for making omelettes, whether for a large group or for one:

1. Use clarified butter instead of whole butter. It will reduce the chance of burning.

2. Use Tabasco sauce instead of pepper. There will be no grains to mar the texture.

3. Use a well-seasoned or non-stick omelette pan. Either season a special omelette pan and hide it so that it is *never* used for any other purpose, or use a pan with a non-stick teflon or silverstone surface.

4. Use a rubber spatula instead of a fork to agitate the eggs in the pan. If you are quick about it (and you have to be quick to make a successful omelette), the spatula barely skims the surface of the pan, agitating the egg more efficiently than a fork, and leaving the non-stick surface unmarred. The spatula also gives you a broader surface to work with when you begin to turn the omelette over itself.

5. Concentrate on what you are doing.

One Perfect Omelette

Serves 1

While most things are easier said than done, omelettes are much easier done than said. You can make an omelette faster than you can read the directions for making one. The perfect omelette should be light and fluffy, creamy on the inside and not browned on the outside, taking less than a minute to prepare.

2-3 large eggs, the fresher the better
1 tablespoon water
⅛ teaspoon (pinch) salt
1-2 drops Tabasco sauce
1 tablespoon clarified butter (see page 23), at room temperature
¼-⅓ cup filling

Mix the eggs lightly with the water, salt and Tabasco. (Mix enough to blend well, but not enough to make the eggs froth.)

Heat the butter in an 8-inch non-stick omelette pan over high heat until it is hot enough for a drop of egg to sizzle. Add the eggs. Wait about 5 seconds, and then begin to build up many layers by agitating the eggs in this manner: Hold a rubber spatula in one hand, and continuously push the eggs from the edge of the pan to the center. At the same time,

grasp the pan handle in your other hand and agitate the pan in a back-and-forth motion so that the loose egg continues to fill in the spaces left as you push the egg with the spatula. When the omelette is set, but still quite moist on top, place the filling at the center.

Start rolling the egg at the point closest to the handle: Using a spatula, lift about a third of the egg up and over the filling, covering about half of it. Reverse your grip on the handle so that your closed fist is palm up. Lift the pan over the serving plate held in your other hand, and by raising the pan in an arc, cause the egg to roll over itself, out of the pan and onto the serving plate.

Forty Perfect Omelettes

Serves 30-40

With practice you can learn to handle two omelette pans simultaneously, which means you can make 40 omelettes in about 20 minutes.

10 dozen large eggs, the fresher the better
2 cups water
2 tablespoons salt, or to taste
½ teaspoon Tabasco sauce, or to taste
3 cups clarified butter, at room temperature

Crack the eggs, one at a time, into a little bowl and then transfer them to several large bowls or containers from which you can measure ounces or cupfuls easily. Whisk to blend. Add the water and whisk to blend. (Strain the eggs, if you want to.) If not using immediately, cover and refrigerate. Just before cooking the omelettes, beat in the salt and Tabasco sauce.

Follow the procedure for making 1 omelette (see previous recipe) 40 times, using 5 to 6 ounces of egg and ¼ to ⅓ cup omelette filling per omelette.

NOTE: Cracking the eggs one at a time into a small bowl is a safety measure—one bad egg can spoil the batch! Also, adding the salt and Tabasco too early can turn the eggs bright orange.

Stir-Fried Oriental Vegetables

Fills 30 omelettes

As in much of Chinese cookery, more time is spent in the preparation of this dish than in the actual cooking. Therefore, much of the work—washing and cutting the vegetables—can be done the day before.

¾ pound snow peas, "strings" removed
1 large bunch broccoli, cut and separated into 2-inch florets
1 pound bean sprouts, beans removed
4 carrots, peeled and sliced in 2-inch julienne strips
1 red pepper, seeded and cut into 2-inch julienne
1 pepper, seeded and cut into 2-inch julienne
4 scallions (with tops), cleaned and thinly sliced
2 8-ounce cans water chestnuts, drained and rinsed
15-ounce can baby corn, drained and rinsed
3 tablespoons peanut oil
3 tablespoons finely chopped fresh ginger
4 tablespoons diced Smithfield ham (optional, but recommended)
1½ tablespoons Oriental sesame oil
Salt, to taste
Freshly ground white pepper, to taste
Garnish: ½ cup sesame seeds, dry-roasted in a hot pan until lightly browned

Rinse and dry the snow peas, broccoli and bean sprouts. Set them aside. (If you are preparing these and the other fresh vegetables—the carrots, peppers and scallions—the day before, bag and refrigerate them until needed.) Slice each of the water chestnuts horizontally into thirds, making 3 thin rounds. Set aside. Slice each of the baby corn cobs on the diagonal into thirds. Set aside.

Bring a large amount of water to a rolling boil. Add salt and stir. Blanch the snow peas in the boiling water for about 10 to 30 seconds and transfer to paper towels to drain. Fan to cool or plunge in cold water to stop cooking. In the same manner, separately blanch each of the other vegetables—the carrots, broccoli, bean sprouts, red, green and yellow peppers—just until they lose their rawness, but are still brightly colored and crisp. Combine all the cooled, blanched vegetables.

Heat 3 tablespoons peanut oil over very high heat in a 12-inch sauté pan or wok. When the oil is hot, add the ginger, scallions, water chestnuts, baby corn and diced ham (if used). Toss to coat with oil and heat through. Add the blanched vegetables and toss to heat through. Add the sesame oil and toss to combine. Immediately transfer the mixture to a serving bowl and serve at room temperature. Season to taste with salt and white pepper. Fill each omelette with about ¼ to ⅓ cup filling and sprinkle sesame seeds on top.

NOTE: Obviously this recipe is only a guideline in selecting vegetables. Use the same technique and flavoring to prepare almost any combination of vegetables, or for just one vegetable, such as asparagus, peeled and sliced on the diagonal. Smithfield ham gives this dish much flavor, so try to use it unless you have dedicated vegetarian guests.

Smoked Salmon in Cream Sauce with Dill

Fills 30 omelettes

This filling usually wins the omelette sweepstakes at parties, sometimes outdistancing the other fillings two-to-one. The white sauce can be made ahead and refrigerated, but do not add the smoked salmon and dill to the reheated sauce until the day of the party. The mixture freezes well and also makes a delicious filling for miniature pastry shells.

8 tablespoons unsalted butter
6½ cups finely chopped Spanish or Bermuda onions (about 2 large)
½ cup all-purpose flour
2½ cups heavy cream
½-1 cup half-and-half or light cream
2½ pounds smoked salmon (Nova Scotia, if possible), thickly sliced and cut into ½-inch squares
½ cup finely snipped (use scissors) fresh dill
¼ teaspoon freshly ground white pepper
¼ teaspoon Tabasco sauce
⅛ teaspoon freshly grated nutmeg
Salt, to taste
Garnish (for omelettes):
1-inch sprigs of fresh dill

Heat the butter in a 12-inch heavy-bottomed saucepan over moderate heat. Add the chopped onions, stir and cover the pan with a tight-fitting lid. Reduce the heat slightly and cook the onions for about 15 minutes to soften. Uncover, raise the heat to medium-high and cook to evaporate most of the moisture. Do not let the onions brown. Sprinkle the flour over them, reduce the heat to low and cook for about 5 minutes, stirring constantly. Add the heavy cream, increase the heat to medium-high and mix well. Cook for about 5 minutes, stirring until the sauce thickens. Reduce the heat slightly and stir in ½ cup half-and-half. Cook about 15 more minutes. Keep warm over very low heat.

Combine the salmon and the chopped dill with the sauce. Season with the white pepper, Tabasco and nutmeg. Taste for salt. (The amount of salt needed depends on the saltiness of the salmon.) If you need to thin the mixture slightly, add additional half-and-half. Adjust the seasoning.

Transfer the filling to a double boiler or chafing dish to keep warm. Fill each omelette with about ¼ to ⅓ cup filling. Garnish the top with a beautiful dill sprig.

Apple and Raisin Compote with Almonds

Fills 30 omelettes

Sweet omelettes are such a treat at parties that eaters who can't make up their minds often have a savory omelette to start and then have a sweet one as a pre-dessert dessert. This apple compote may be made several days ahead and refrigerated. Simply rewarm it before serving.

4-6 lemons
24 medium-size apples (Golden
  Delicious are good)
½ pound unsalted butter
1½ teaspoons ground cinnamon,
  freshly ground, if possible
1 teaspoon freshly grated
  nutmeg
3 cups superfine sugar
1½ cups golden raisins
1 cup dark rum
¼ pound (about 1 cup)
  sliced almonds, toasted in a
  350-degree oven until golden
  brown and then cooled to room
  temperature

Either use 2 heavy-bottomed 12-inch sauté pans with tight-fitting lids *or* use 1 pan (as indicated) and repeat the procedure twice.

Squeeze the lemons. Measure 6 tablespoons of juice and set aside. Pour the remaining juice into a large bowl of cold water to make acidulated water. Peel and core the apples. Cut each into about 12 wedges and place them in the water.

Heat half the butter in a large sauté pan. Add half the cinnamon, nutmeg, sugar, raisins and reserved lemon juice to the pan. Drain half of the apple wedges and add them to the pan. Cover and cook over moderate heat until the apples are soft but not mushy.

Pour the contents of the pan into a strainer held over a bowl. Reserve the drained apples and raisins. Return the syrup to the pan. Add half the rum and stir to combine. Cook over high heat until the syrup reduces, thickens and caramelizes. Combine the syrup with the cooked apples and raisins. Repeat this procedure with the second half of the ingredients and combine the two.

Place the apple filling in a double boiler or chafing dish to keep warm. Fill each omelette with about ¼ to ⅓ cup filling. Decorate the top with toasted sliced almonds.

Basic French Crêpes

Makes 14-16 6-inch crêpes

Omelettes are a fluffy, satisfying cloak for a filling, while crêpes are a thinner, more delicate one. Should you decide that crêpes are exactly what you need, here is a fool-proof recipe.

1 cup Wondra flour
⅔ cup milk
⅔ cup water
3 large eggs
¼ teaspoon salt
3 tablespoons clarified butter,
  (see page 23), melted and
  cooled, plus a small amount
  to grease crêpe pan

Process all the ingredients in a food processor (or blender) until smooth. Let rest for at least 20 minutes.

Brush a 6-inch crêpe pan with a small amount of clarified butter. (This step is usually only necessary for the first crêpe.) Heat the pan over medium-high heat until a drop of water just sizzles upon contact. Pour about ¼ cup of the batter into the pan, swirl quickly to cover the pan bottom and pour out the excess. Cook until the edges begin to brown slightly (about 30 seconds). Flip the crêpe and cook the other side for about 15 to 20 seconds.

Bacon-Wrapped Bananas, Prunes and Oysters

Makes 90 pieces

Bacon-wrapped tidbits are standard hors d'oeuvres that go into and out of fashion as often as designer dresses. Judging by current response, they are in. Partially cooking the bacon produces a better result— the centers don't get cremated. Choose one, or all three of the tidbits recommended for wrapping. If you're having 30 guests, you will probably want to serve one of each kind.

45 strips thinly sliced bacon
30 raw oysters, drained and
   dried with paper towel
30 medium-size pitted prunes
4-6 ripe but firm bananas
   cut into 30 1-inch-thick
   slices
Juice of 1 lemon

Preheat the oven to 350 degrees. Separate the bacon slices and set them on several baking sheets in a single layer. Bake until they just begin to brown. (They should be flexible enough to roll.) Transfer to paper towels to drain. Continue until all the bacon is partially cooked in this manner. Cut each slice in half.

Raise the oven temperature to 450 degrees. Roll each oyster in a bacon strip, secure with a toothpick and place on a rack over a broiler pan. The bacon edges should be on the bottom. Bake until the bacon is crisp and the oysters are cooked. Drain and serve hot. Follow this same procedure with the prunes.

Toss the bananas with the lemon juice to coat. Follow the above procedure.

NOTE: Occasionally an oyster may be too large. If so, cut it in half. Also, while this recipe suggests medium-size prunes, you may prefer to use large ones.

Mixed Green Salad with Julienne of Swiss Cheese and Endive

Serves 30

3-4 pounds assorted salad greens
   (approximately)
1 pound Swiss Gruyère cheese
6 Belgian endives
3 cups Creamy Vinaigrette
   Dressing (see page 26)

Cut or break the salad greens into bite-sized pieces. Wash well in cold water and dry in a salad spinner. Cut the cheese into thin julienne strips (about 2 inches long) with a sharp, thin-bladed knife. Cut away the root end and bitter core of the endives. Wash and dry the leaves. Cut lengthwise into thin julienne, about the same size as the cheese.

Place the greens in a large salad bowl. Sprinkle the endive strips around the perimeter and the cheese strips at the center. Toss at the table with the dressing.

Pound Cake and Fresh Strawberries
with Chocolate Fondue

Serves 30

This is theoretically finger food, but for the sake of your carpet (as well as your guests' shirts), we do recommend small plates. Bake the pound cakes a day or two ahead. Before serving, cut into cubes, and have toothpicks or tiny wooden forks nearby for dunking them into the fondue. The adventurous may dunk the strawberries by their stems.

POUND CAKE

Makes 2 loaves

**¾ pound unsalted butter,
plus butter for greasing pans,
at room temperature**
**3 cups flour, plus flour for
dusting pans**
1 tablespoon baking powder
2 teaspoons vanilla extract
½ teaspoon almond extract
¾ cup half-and-half
2¼ cups sugar
**6 large eggs, at room
temperature**

For the pound cake: Preheat the oven to 350 degrees. Butter 2 5½-by-9-inch loaf pans. Line the bottoms with wax paper, butter the paper and flour the pans lightly.

Sift the flour and baking powder together. Add the vanilla and almond extracts to the half-and-half in a separate bowl. Cream the butter and sugar together with an electric mixer until light and fluffy. Scrape down the sides of the bowl, as necessary, throughout the process. Add the eggs, one at a time, and mix at low speed to incorporate. Add the flour mixture and the half-and-half alternately to the creamed butter and sugar mixture, beginning and ending with the flour mixture. Mix at high speed until smooth, but do not overbeat. Divide the batter between the loaf pans. Smooth the tops with a spatula and tap the pans lightly on a counter to settle. Bake for 1 hour, or until the cake pulls away from the sides of the pan.

Remove from the oven and cool in the pans on a rack for about 30 minutes. Unmold and let cool completely. Wrap the cakes in plastic wrap and refrigerate overnight. (Pound cake tastes better the second day.) Cut them into uniform 1-inch cubes to serve.

CHOCOLATE FONDUE

18 ounces Toblerone bittersweet
   chocolate, broken into pieces
½-¾ cup heavy cream
¼ cup Cognac
6 pints fresh strawberries,
   (with stems on if possible),
   wiped clean (or quickly
   rinsed and dried), at
   room temperature

For the chocolate fondue: Melt the chocolate in the top of a double boiler over hot (but not boiling) water. Stir until smooth. Add ½ cup cream in a steady stream, stirring with a whisk, and heat through. Add the Cognac and stir to combine. If the mixture is too thick, stir in more cream as needed (but do not make the mixture too thin—it must coat the fruit and not run off).

Keep the fondue warm in a double boiler or in a fondue pot. Serve accompanied by platters of fresh strawberries and cubes of pound cake. Have toothpicks and cocktail napkins at hand along with small bread and butter plates, if desired.

NOTE: If fresh strawberries are not available or too expensive, substitute firm, ripe bananas cut into 1-inch chunks. (In that case, do not serve bacon-wrapped bananas as an hors d'oeuvre.)

Grapes Juanita

Serves 24

An easy, delicious dessert with one important proviso: the grapes must be sweet, not puckery.

1½ cups instantized brown sugar
2 1-by-3-inch strips orange peel,
   dried and finely chopped
6 pounds green seedless grapes,
   stemmed, washed and dried
3 cups sour cream
3 navel oranges, cut into rounds

Place the brown sugar and orange peel in a food processor fitted with the steel blade and process until the peel is completely incorporated into the sugar. Combine the orange sugar with the sour cream and fold into the grapes. Chill. Serve in a large bowl decorated with orange slices, or in individual wine goblets with a round of orange perched on each rim.

NOTE: You may use the orange peel fresh or dried. If you are mixing fresh peel with the sugar, you must use it the same day; if you use dried peel, you can store the orange sugar for some time before using. To dry orange peel, leave it in a sunny spot for a day, or until it is completely dried.

A Menu for an Expandable Holiday Buffet for 50–100: Celebrate America

HORS D'OEUVRES

*Crudités (Raw Vegetables of Your Choice),
with *Creamy Avocado Dip • Green Goddess Dip (page 38)
*New Delhi Dip with Yogurt and Fresh Coriander

Raw Oyster Bar with Golden American Caviar,
or
Sides of Western Smoked Salmon
with Black Bread,
or
Crabmeat Mousse
(page 37)

ENTREES

*Baked Holiday Ham

*Cheese Biscuits • Assorted Mustards

*Hopping John • *Southern Spoon Bread

*Breast of Smoked Turkey with Horseradish Mayonnaise
Buttered, Thinly Sliced Rye Bread, or Freshly Made Small Buns
*Cranberry-Apple Compote with Applejack, or
Warm Apple and Raisin Compote with Almonds (page 52)

*Broccoli with Garlic Oil • *Spinach Salad with Marinated Mushrooms
Tortellini Primavera (page 84)

Assorted American Cheeses and Fruits in Season (page 83)

DESSERTS

*Rice Pudding with Golden Raisins, with Red Raspberry Sauce (page 43)

Chocolate Mousse (page 81)

*International Coffee Specialties
with Cordials of Your Choice

PARTY DRINKS

*Lake Water • Chilled Beer
White Wine • Red Wine

Setting Up Your Home for a Large Party

Where to Put the People

Entertaining a large number of people is no small challenge. Careful planning is the key to success. We suggest not only that you think everything out; but also that you write it down, even to the point of diagramming where your food will go on the buffet table.

When planning for large groups, look at your home objectively as a series of spaces for people to gather. Living and dining areas are obvious party spaces, but what about the entrance foyer? kitchen? outdoor deck? garden? den? bedroom?

Decide where you want your guests to congregate, and plan interest areas—for food, drink, music, entertainment—in those spaces. For example, for a large indoor holiday buffet, you will most likely use the dining room as the central food area. You will probably set up two bars (see page 14), perhaps the first at one side of the living room, the second in the den or kitchen. (We've even set up bars in very large closets.) You may also decide to have dance music in the living room. Perhaps you will set up small tables for dining on an outdoor deck, or even in a large entrance foyer. During the party, these interest areas will become focal points for activity, and landmarks to guide your guests in the circulation patterns you wish them to follow.

Where to Put the Furniture

Do not attempt to provide table seating for 50 to 100 people—you are not a restaurant. You may decide to rent some tables and chairs to create dining areas; but don't feel obligated to place everyone at table. Guests will find places to sit, if they so desire, and they will also cope quite well with their food and drink. (One of the most elegant parties we've ever catered, in a New York City penthouse, was just such a casual affair. Many of the guests, almost all of whom seemed to be members of the British aristocracy, ensconced themselves quite comfortably on the plush green living-room carpet, so that the room looked remarkably like an impromptu picnic on a fashionable English lawn.)

Do not banish all your furniture to a bedroom. A common misconception is that party rooms must be vast open spaces, devoid of furniture. A room cleared of furniture is a room cleared of character. You may want to clear a space for a dance floor, and perhaps for several smaller dining areas, and you may have to rearrange your dining room to serve the buffet (see below)—but otherwise, leave your furniture in place. If you find your home comfortable, so will your guests. (There are, of course, exceptions to this rule. We recently catered a wedding for 100 in a space that would only hold 50. Furniture had to be moved back against the walls as well as into a bedroom. It was a squeeze, but it worked.)

You may wish to set up some folding chairs for additional seating as well as folding snack tables (both are rentable), but be judicious. Don't make your home look like a furniture store or a theater in the round.

Where to Put the Food

PLACING THE BUFFET TABLE

In most cases, the logical place for the buffet table is the dining room. For easy access to the table remove all dining-room chairs (place them against the walls or in other rooms). Leave the table at the center of the room if it is large enough for guests to circulate freely around the buffet. In a small dining room, it is advisable to move the table close to a wall, leaving only enough space for you, or any servers, to stand behind. (If your dining table is too small, rent a larger table to use for the buffet and place your dining table against a far wall, perhaps set up for coffee service.)

An alternate approach is to have several food stations arranged throughout the party space. The most obvious example is to utilize an outdoor grill, in season, to expand both the menu and the party space. But whatever the season, all the food for your party need not be in one place. Arrange platters of crudités or assorted cheeses at the bars. Set up a fresh oyster bar in the kitchen (fill an extra sink with crushed ice and oysters). Plan a beautiful dessert table, separate but visible from the buffet (so people can see—and save room for—dessert). Set another table for coffee service and perhaps with an assortment of cordials. Separating the food in this way also separates the crowd and avoids that old party bugaboo—congestion!

ARRANGING THE BUFFET TABLE

When planning the setup of the buffet, role-play as a guest. Place things in logical order, starting with plates, forks and napkins (we often roll the napkin and fork together, and tie with colorful ribbon). *Arrange the food in the order you would normally plate it to serve.* Place the "main course" items, with their accompaniments, first: the Baked Holiday Ham with Cheese Biscuits and the Breast of Smoked Turkey with its Cranberry-Apple Compote. Next place the vegetables, side dishes and salads: the Hopping John, Spoon Bread, Broccoli in Garlic Oil and Spinach Salad.

Finally place the cheese and fruit and, if desired, the dessert. (As noted, you may decide on a separate dessert table.)

What you are setting up is called a "food station." For a small group, set up one food station and have people move in one direction around the table. For larger groups, set up two identical food stations so that people can go in two directions at once. In general one food station can feed 25 people, two can feed 50, etc. For 100 people, set up two separate buffet tables, with two food stations each.

Obviously these food arrangements and traffic patterns must be planned ahead, but good planning will save the embarrassment of having lines of people form at the buffet.

WRITING IT DOWN

We strongly suggest that you make diagrams for placement of food on the buffet table and for placement of furniture around your home. These drawings will enable you to delegate some of the setting-up responsibilities to assistants. Otherwise you will have to do everything yourself, and for a large party there is simply too much to do.

What to Serve

• Choose fork food or finger food only. No knives should be needed at a buffet.
• Cold and room-temperature food is preferable. Cooking food for 50 to 100 people in a home kitchen is not easy.
• Keep hot foods warm in chafing dishes set over hot water. Choose items that hold well over heat.
• Plan the menu around items that can be made ahead, in whole or in part.
• Utilize convenience foods, if you like. Buy good breads from a good bakery. Supplement your menu with items purchased at a fancy food take-out shop, and season them to your taste.
• Avoid highly perishable foods, such as custard sauces or raw meats or fish, unless you can control their temperatures and presentation.

• Choose foods for a variety of tastes, textures and colors.
• Don't put all the food out at once. Have back-up trays of food ready to replace dwindling ones at the buffet.
• When purchasing large quantities of food you can often get a discount. Ask, and ye shall receive.
• Plan one or two items for visual impact at the buffet: bushel baskets of apples; crates of grapes. An opulent display of one food makes a design impact, and is often not overly expensive. A huge bowl of fresh strawberries in season, for example, is a far less costly centerpiece than one floral display—and a better tasting one!
• Plan a kitchen production schedule (see page 17).
• Plan for storage space. You might have to use a friend's refrigerator to supplement your own.

The menu we suggest for a holiday buffet follows the rules outlined above. The main course items—smoked turkey and ham—are both purchased fully cooked. The ham is glazed and baked the morning of the party and may be served at room temperature. The Cranberry-Apple Compote actually tastes better if made the day before. The Hopping John may be made ahead and rewarmed before it goes in its chafing dish, or served as a salad. The broccoli is blanched ahead and coated with garlic oil just before serving. Only the Spoon Bread and Cheese Biscuits require any last-minute attention.

The spinach for the salad can be carefully washed and dried a day or two ahead and refrigerated in large plastic bags with a paper towel in each to absorb excess moisture. (This is true of any salad green.) The spinach is then tossed with dressing just before serving. The crudités receive similar treatment (see page 70), and all of the dips can be made a day ahead.

Even the Rice Pudding and its Red Raspberry Sauce can be made ahead and served well chilled.

Expanding the Buffet

If you invite 100 people to your holiday buffet, expecting 50 to accept, what do you do when 102 acceptances pour in? You bask in your popularity and plan ways to expand the buffet.

Some suggestions:
- Ask guests to bring food. A covered-dish party is fun, and in the current vogue of reverse snobbery, quite chic.
- Prepare more quantities of the same food, four hams instead of two, etc.

- Expand the menu by setting up other food stations. Some ideas:

A pasta bar, offering guests a choice of sauces to toss into hot pasta.

A taco bar, offering a choice of toppings: chili con carne, cheeses, salsa, etc.

A sundae bar, for making fantasy ice cream desserts.

An omelette or crêpe station (see page 46).

A mixed grill, out at the old bar-b-que.

The Bar (see page 13)

Lake Water (A PARTY DRINK)   *Recipe makes 1*

When we do menu consultations for restaurants, we often develop a "signature" drink for the menu. This one was developed for a restaurant in Massachusetts on the shores of Lake Chargoggagoggman-chauggagoggchaubunagungamaugg. For obvious reasons, we call it Lake Water. The drink is a shockingly bright blue color and a certain conversation starter at parties. It is particularly suited to warm weather, but its bright blue color makes it a shoo-in for any red-white-and-blue American buffet.

Ice cubes
1 ounce vodka
1 ounce Bols Blue Curacao
Tonic water
Wedge of lemon

Fill a 12-ounce wine goblet or glass (double old-fashioned) about three-quarters full with ice cubes. Add the vodka and Blue Curacao. Fill to the top with tonic water. Squeeze the lemon into the drink, stir and serve.

NOTE: Blue Curacao is available in some liquor stores, but not all. It has the same mildly orange flavor as Curacao. To alleviate your suspicions, the bright blue color is indeed from food coloring. Bols is the brand we recommend.

Southern Spoon Bread

Serves 60 at a buffet

This is our version of a traditional Southern recipe. We use yellow cornmeal because we like the color, canned creamed corn because we like the texture, and baking powder (instead of egg whites) because it's much too hectic at a party to whip and fold in egg whites properly. In the South, they gild this golden lily with butter. Why not?

8 tablespoons (¼ pound) unsalted butter, plus butter to grease pan
2½ quarts milk
1 pound yellow cornmeal
1½ tablespoons salt
2 tablespoons sugar
1 teaspoon freshly grated nutmeg
2 cups (17-ounce can) creamed corn
2 cups water
12 large eggs
¼ teaspoon Tabasco sauce
2 tablespoons double-acting baking powder
Optional accompaniment: unsalted butter, at room temperature

Preheat the oven to 325 degrees. Lightly butter a 2-by-12-by-20-inch baking pan (or 2 half-size pans, each 2 by 10 by 12 inches).

Bring the butter and milk just to a simmer in a large heavy-bottomed saucepan, stirring constantly to avoid scorching. Mix the cornmeal, salt, sugar and nutmeg together in a large mixing bowl. Add the creamed corn and water, whisking well to blend. Stir this mixture into the hot milk. Cook until thickened, stirring constantly. Remove from the heat and cool slightly.

Whisk the eggs with the Tabasco sauce to blend. Add the baking powder and whisk to blend again. Whisk a small amount of the hot cornmeal mixture into the beaten eggs to warm them, then whisk the warm eggs into the hot cornmeal mixture, blending well.

Pour the batter into the baking pan and bake for about 50 minutes or until the top is lightly browned and a knife inserted into the center of the spoon bread comes out clean.

Serve at once, using a serving spoon. (Place the baking pan in a chafing dish insert to keep warm over hot water.) Have a tub of unsalted butter nearby, at room temperature.

NOTE: The baking pan suggested for this recipe (2 by 12 by 20 inches) is also known as a "hotel pan." If you are renting a chafing dish for your party, rent this size insert for your chafing dish.

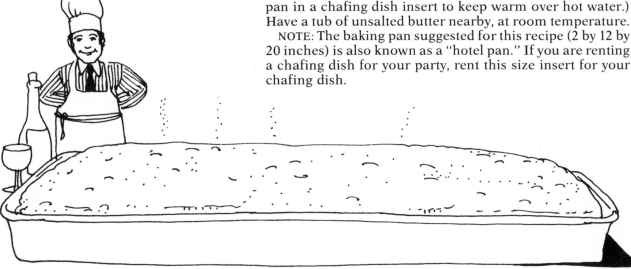

Baked Holiday Ham

2 hams—serves 50

We are about to divulge a secret: the recipe for a sweet, smoky, succulent, tender, lean and delicous ham we serve at parties. What could be more American than a ham from the heartland—Dubuque, Iowa—basted in beer and brown sugar? For 50 people, bake two hams; for 100, three or four. Bake ahead, and serve the hams warm or at room temperature.

2 12- to 16-pound smoked hams, boneless or semi-boneless (fully cooked and smoked), preferably Dubuque Fleur de Lis brand
Glaze: (for 2 hams)
1 pound box dark brown sugar
½ cup prepared Dijon mustard
½ teaspoon ground cloves
½-¾ cup beer
Whole cloves to stud hams
Garnish: fresh kale, washed and dried, tough stems removed

Preheat the oven to 350 degrees. Unwrap one ham and blot to remove any excess moisture. Place, fat side up, in a shallow roasting pan. Bake for 1¼ hours. While it is baking, make the glaze. Mix the sugar with the mustard and ground cloves. Add ½ cup beer and as much additional beer as necessary to make a smooth thick paste which can be brushed on the ham. (The moisture content of brown sugar may vary, so add beer accordingly.) Divide the glaze, using half for each ham.

Remove the ham from the oven. Cut away the rind and excess fat, as necessary. Leave a thin layer of fat over the surface, if possible. Score the top, cutting lightly through the fat in a diamond pattern, and place a whole clove at each corner. Brush the glaze generously over the ham, reserving a small amount for basting.

Return the ham to the oven and bake another 45 minutes, basting with glaze every 15 minutes. The internal temperature of the ham should reach 130 degrees on a meat thermometer. If necessary to brown the glaze further, place the ham under the broiler, if there is room, or raise the oven temperature to the hottest setting and bake an additional 15 minutes.

Remove the ham from the oven and let it rest at least 15 minutes before serving, or serve at room temperature. Decorate the base with fresh kale—it looks attractive and doesn't wilt quickly. Slice the ham to order, because if cut ahead, the slices dry out very quickly.

Repeat this whole process with the second ham.

Hopping John

We were introduced to this dish years ago by Larry Blyden, the late and sorely missed actor, television personality and true Southern gentleman. We catered several New Year's Day open houses for him that featured this dish, traditionally served on New Year's Day in the South as a symbol of good luck. We often serve it now at weddings to wish the bride and groom good luck—though we do stop short of throwing it at them as they leave.

Hopping John, served hot, makes an excellent, contrasting accompaniment to the ham. If you like, you can also make it into a salad to serve at a summer wedding by cooling the Hopping John without the parsley and bacon garnishes. Just before serving, add the parsley and bacon, along with 12 thinly sliced scallions, a 12-ounce jar of pimientos, drained and diced, and 4 finely chopped shallot. Toss well with 2 cups Quantity Vinaigrette Dressing (see page 68) and serve at room temperature.

2 pounds dried black-eyed peas
1 ham hock plus ham bone, if available
1 pound thick cut double-smoked bacon (reserve the rind)
1 pound long-grain Carolina rice
8 medium-size onions, finely chopped
4 packets instant chicken bouillon
Salt, to taste
Black pepper, to taste
1 cup chopped parsley

Soak the black-eyed peas in water for 4 hours (or follow the package instructions for soaking). Boil the ham hock, ham bone and bacon rind about 1 hour until tender. Cook the rice according to the instructions on page 28.

Cook the bacon in a large sauté pan over moderate heat until crisp. Remove it, drain and set aside. Remove 2 tablespoons bacon fat from the pan and reserve. Add the onions to the pan and cook until softened and lightly browned. Reserve them together with the bacon fat in which they were cooked.

Drain the black-eyed peas and place them in a large saucepan with the ham hock and bone, the bacon rind and enough fresh water to cover by about 2 inches. Add the 2 tablespoons reserved bacon fat and the 4 packets instant chicken bouillon. Bring to a boil, reduce the heat and simmer, skimming the surface occasionally, until the peas are tender (about 25 to 35 minutes). Remove the ham hock and set it aside. Remove and discard the ham bone and bacon rind. Drain the cooked peas.

Trim the meat from the ham hock, dice it and combiné it with the black-eyed peas, rice and the onions in their bacon fat. Add salt and black pepper to taste and half the chopped parsley. Toss gently to combine.

Dice the reserved crisp bacon. Place the Hopping John in a serving pan or bowl and garnish the top with the bacon and remaining chopped parsley. The Hopping John can be kept warm over steam in a chafing dish.

Cheese Biscuits

Makes 12 biscuits

If there is a better partner for a slice of baked ham than this biscuit, we haven't found it. Although the recipe makes 12 biscuits, they divide easily in half to make 24 plump little open-faced ham sandwiches. Biscuits never taste as good when reheated, so if you have enough help in the kitchen, continue to make fresh ones throughout the party. Otherwise, make them ahead and reheat in a warm oven.

2 cups flour, plus extra for dusting board, rolling pin and biscuit cutter
½ teaspoon salt
1 tablespoon baking powder
½ teaspoon baking soda
5 tablespoons unsalted butter:
  3 tablespoons chilled,
  2 tablespoons melted
⅔ cup grated Parmesan cheese
1 cup buttermilk (or sour milk—see Note)

Preheat the oven to 450 degrees. Sift the flour, salt, baking powder and baking soda together into a mixing bowl. Add 3 tablespoons chilled butter and cut it in with a pastry cutter or 2 knives until the mixture resembles coarse crumbs. Add the grated cheese and toss to blend well. Make a well in the center of the flour mixture and pour in the buttermilk. Quickly incorporate the liquid with a fork until the dough starts to come together.

Turn the dough out onto a lightly floured board, form it into a ball with your hands and knead about 10 turns, until the dough holds together. (Do not overknead or the biscuits will be tough.) Roll the dough with a lightly floured rolling pin until it is about ¼ inch thick.

Dip a 2-inch biscuit cutter into the flour and cut the dough into rounds. (Do not turn the cutter, but rather cut straight down.) Place half the biscuit rounds on a non-stick baking sheet. Brush the tops with melted butter, and place a second biscuit round on top of each. Brush the tops with butter. Bake for 12 to 15 minutes or until the biscuits are browned.

NOTE: To make 1 cup sour milk, add 2 tablespoons vinegar to 1 cup milk and allow the mixture to stand for 30 minutes before using.

Breast of Smoked Turkey with Horseradish Mayonnaise

Serves 50 at a buffet

There is a resurgence of independent smokehouses across America, smoking everything from mullet to mallard, from baby lamb to tom turkey. Make an effort to find good smoked turkey—not too salty, wet or gelatinous—and slice it by hand as thinly as possible. (Machine-made slices are too thin and too big to be effective.) Serve the turkey and mayonnaise with thin slices of rye bread, buttered, or delicate little buns.

1-3 tablespoons prepared
  horseradish sauce, or to taste
4 cups mayonnaise
½ cup finely chopped fresh
  chives or parsley, plus
  some for garnish
3 2- to 3-pound breasts smoked
  turkey (6-9 pounds in all)*

Add the prepared horseradish sauce to the mayonnaise, 1 tablespoon at a time, until the desired degree of hotness is achieved. Fold in the chopped chives. Divide between several small serving bowls. Cover and refrigerate.

Hand-slice the smoked turkey into very thin, biscuit-sized pieces.

Set a serving bowl of horseradish mayonnaise at the center of a round serving platter and garnish it with chopped chives. Arrange the smoked turkey slices in a decorative overlapping pattern to encircle the bowl. Prepare several trays of smoked turkey in this manner. Cover them and keep refrigerated until ready to serve.

*Having tried many varieties, we recommend Pollack's Hickory-Smoked Boneless Turkey Breast, which is available in the New York area, or by mail order from: A. & N. Pollack, Inc., 638 West 131st Street, New York, NY 10027 (212-281-9111).

Cranberry Apple Compote with Applejack

Makes 6 cups

If you are cranberryless, serve the warm Apple and Raisin Compote on page 52. Next year, store some bags of cranberries in your freezer. They freeze well.

1¼ cups sugar
1 cup water
¼ cup orange juice
1½ pounds Granny Smith apples,
  peeled, cored and cut into
  ¼-inch dice
3 cups cranberries (12-ounce
  bag), washed and picked over
½ tablespoon minced orange rind
¼ teaspoon freshly ground
  cinnamon

Bring the sugar, water and orange juice to a boil in a heavy-bottomed saucepan. Reduce the heat and simmer for 5 minutes. Add the apples and return to the boil, then reduce the heat again and cook for another 5 minutes, stirring occasionally. Pour the apples and liquid through a strainer held over a bowl. Return the syrup to the saucepan and set the apples aside in a large bowl.

Add the cranberries to the syrup and bring to a boil. Reduce the heat and cook for about 7 minutes, stirring occasionally, until the cranberries burst. Strain the mixture over a bowl, being careful not to crush the cranberries, and

¼ teaspoon allspice
2 tablespoons Applejack
brandy
4-5 ounces walnuts, shelled
½-¾ cup superfine sugar

reserve the syrup. Add the cranberries to the apples. Return the cranberry-apple syrup to the saucepan and boil for about 3 to 5 minutes to thicken. Pour it back over the fruit. Add all the remaining ingredients (except the superfine sugar) and stir to blend. Stir in ½ cup of the superfine sugar, taste and add more sugar, if desired. Cool, stirring occasionally, and refrigerate.

Broccoli with Garlic Oil

Serves 24

10 pounds (about 5 or 6 bunches)
fresh broccoli
5 cloves garlic
1 cup olive oil
Salt, to taste
Cayenne pepper, to taste

Cut off the woody bottoms of the broccoli stems. Separate the spears, leaving them attached to the florets. Peel the stalks as necessary. Soak the broccoli in lightly salted cold water for 10 minutes, while you bring a large quantity of salted water to a rapid boil (see page 25). Blanch the broccoli in the boiling water in batches, just until you can insert a paring knife into the stalk easily. Do not overcook—the broccoli should be bright green. Fan to cool, or plunge in cold water to stop cooking. (The broccoli can be blanched a day ahead and refrigerated; bring to room temperature before dressing with the garlic oil.)

To make the garlic oil, lightly smash the garlic cloves with the flat heel of a chef's knife. Remove the skins and discard. Place the olive oil and garlic in a 12-inch, heavy-bottomed sauté pan. Heat over high heat until bubbles appear around the garlic. Reduce the heat and fry the cloves, turning them constantly with a long-handled slotted spoon, until they are light brown (do not allow the garlic to burn; it will make the oil bitter). Discard the garlic and, if necessary, strain the oil. Cool slightly and season to taste with salt and cayenne pepper.

Arrange the broccoli spears decoratively in a serving bowl, floret ends up. Brush generously with the warm oil and serve at room temperature.

Spinach Salad with Marinated Mushrooms

Serves 50 at a buffet

Spinach salad holds up very well at a buffet because dressed spinach leaves do not wilt as quickly as other salad greens. We recommend dressing and serving only half the salad at a time. Marinate the mushrooms just enough to take away their rawness, but not enough to turn them soggy and brown.

**6 pounds fresh spinach
(approximately)**
**2 quarts Quantity Vinaigrette
Dressing (see page 68)**
**3 pounds (1 basket) fresh
mushrooms, preferably large**
Garnish: ½ cup chopped parsley

Wash the spinach carefully in at least 3 changes of cold water to remove all grit. Remove and discard any tough stems. Tear the leaves into bite-size pieces. Drain well and refrigerate in a plastic bag until ready to serve.

Make the quantity vinaigrette dressing recipe twice. Pour about 3 cups of it into a large bowl to marinate the mushrooms and reserve the rest.

Clean the mushrooms by wiping them with damp paper towels or, if it is necessary to wash them, rinsing them quickly under cold running water, then wiping dry. (Mushrooms absorb water like a sponge, so don't soak them.) Cut off the tips of the stems, slice the mushrooms thinly through the caps and stems, tossing the slices in the bowl of dressing as you go. Marinate, tossing periodically, for about 1 hour at room temperature. (If necessary, add up to 1 more cup dressing.) Drain the mushrooms and discard any liquid.

To serve: Toss half the spinach with enough dressing to coat. Place half the marinated mushrooms at the center and garnish with chopped parsley. Repeat to serve the second half of the salad.

Quantity Vinaigrette Dressing

Makes 1 quart

By far the easiest method for making a large quantity of salad dressing is to put everything into a blender or food processor and whiz away! In this recipe, the egg yolk and the action of the blender "whip" the salad dressing and give it a creamy color and consistency. This dressing has a high proportion of vinegar to oil, which makes it piquant; you will need less than usual to dress a salad.

2½ cups salad oil
1½ cups red wine vinegar
1 tablespoon dried tarragon,
   preferably French
1 egg yolk
1 teaspoon salt, or to taste
Freshly ground black pepper,
   to taste
4 drops Tabasco sauce, or to
   taste
4 garlic cloves, chopped

Put all the ingredients in a blender or food processor and mix well.

NOTES: When mixing dressing with salad greens, particularly a large quantity, *never* add all of the dressing at once. Add it in stages, tossing to blend and tasting as you go. You can always add more dressing, but you can't salvage a soggy salad. Use just enough dressing to coat the greens lightly. It is also a good idea to taste the salad for seasoning before serving and add salt and freshly ground pepper to taste.

This is a basic recipe that can be altered to taste by varying the kinds of oil or vinegar used and by adding or substituting various herbs and flavorings.

Rice Pudding with Golden Raisins
Serves 30

Certain foods recall the security of childhood, with all its warmth and comfort. Rice pudding is such a dish. We consider it a classic American dessert. It does to us what Madeleines did to Proust.

4 quarts milk
2¼ cups sugar (divided to
   make 1½ cups and ¾ cup)
3-inch stick cinnamon
Peel of ½ lemon
1 pound Carolina rice
1¼ teaspoons salt
1 cup soft golden raisins
4 eggs
3 tablespoons cornstarch
Powdered cinnamon, freshly
   ground if possible
Optional accompaniments:
   Heavy cream
   Softly whipped cream, lightly
   flavored with confectioners'
   sugar and vanilla
   Red Raspberry Sauce
   (see page 43)

Bring the milk, 1½ cups sugar, the cinnamon stick and lemon peel to a boil in a heavy-bottomed 8-quart saucepan over high heat, stirring to prevent scorching. Slowly sprinkle in the rice and ¼ teaspoon salt. Return to the boil, reduce the heat and simmer, stirring constantly, until the rice has almost cooked. Add the raisins and continue to simmer until the rice is tender. Discard the cinnamon stick and lemon peel.

Mix the eggs with the remaining sugar and then with the cornstarch. Whisk to blend. Gradually spoon about 1 cup of the hot rice mixture into the beaten eggs, whisking constantly. Pour the warm egg mixture back into the rice in the pan and stir to blend. Bring the pudding to a boil, stirring constantly. Remove from the heat and cool, stirring occasionally. If storing in the refrigerator, place a piece of plastic wrap directly onto the surface of the pudding to prevent a "skin" from forming. Sprinkle with cinnamon before serving.

NOTE: Rice pudding may be served warm, at room temperature or chilled. For an All-American color scheme, serve it with Red Raspberry Sauce.

Creamy Avocado Dip

1 pound onions, peeled and
  coarsely chopped
2 cloves garlic, peeled and
  coarsely chopped
7-8 ripe avocados
¼ cup lemon juice
1 pint sour cream
Fresh horseradish, to taste
Salt, to taste
Tabasco sauce, to taste

Peel the avocados, dice the flesh and toss in lemon juice. Place in a food processor fitted with the steel blade, add the remaining ingredients and process to blend. (You may have to do this in two batches.) Refrigerate the dip in a covered container until well chilled, for several hours or overnight.

New Delhi Dip

Makes 3 cups

1 tablespoon ground cumin
3 tablespoons finely chopped
  onion
¾ teaspoon salt, or to taste
3 tablespoons finely chopped fresh
  coriander (cilantro), or parsley
3 tablespoons finely chopped
  fresh mint leaves (optional)
Dash sugar (optional)
1½ cups mayonnaise
1½ cups plain yogurt

Toast the cumin in an ungreased skillet over low heat for 30 seconds. Add to the mayonnaise along with the onion, salt, coriander and mint, if using, and blend well. Fold the mayonnaise mixture into the yogurt. Refrigerate the dip for at least 1 hour before serving.

Crudités and Dips

Once, upon our arrival in the kitchen of a mansion where we were to cater a dinner party, we encountered the family cook whose services had been supplanted for the evening. "Harrumph!" she snorted, watching us unpack carefully bagged crudités that had taken most of a day to carve, "*my* carrot sticks are better!"

Everyone serves crudités and everyone dips; so how do you make yours special?
• Buy only very fresh, unblemished vegetables—not more than one day before the party.
• Wash and trim them. Cut each vegetable into exact uniform size. This quality control separates the crudes from the crudités.
• Refresh cut vegetables in ice water. Drain well and seal in plastic bags with a paper towel inside to absorb excess moisture.
• Arrange your veggies artfully and serve at once, with a small dish of sea salt and a choice of unusual and delicious dips. You may have your own candidates in the dip department; here are ours .

COFFEE FOR A CROWD

There is a truism in the restaurant business that coffee must be very good because it is often the last lingering taste one has of a restaurant meal. The same is true for parties.

How to Make Coffee for a Crowd

- Use the correct amount of coffee. One pound of coffee makes 42 5-ounce servings. (For good, rich coffee we use 1 pound of coffee to 6½ quarts of water.)
- Use good fresh coffee. It can be freshly ground from the bean or taken from a freshly opened can—but it must be fresh.
- Use a clean coffee maker and fresh cold water.
- Remove the grounds as soon as the coffee is brewed.
- Don't let brewed coffee *ever* boil. Keep a lid on to avoid evaporation. Keep the coffee warm at a constant, even temperature.
- No matter what brewing method you use or what method of keeping the pot warm, coffee deteriorates after about an hour.
- If you rent a coffee maker, make certain you understand how it works before putting it to use.

Special Coffee Drinks

The addition of liqueurs or brandy to coffee can make this everyday drink into a party delight. You *must* start with good strong coffee or espresso (some brands can be brewed in any kind of coffee maker), then add the liqueur of choice, to taste. Sweeten, if necessary, and top with lightly whipped cream, if you wish.

You can arrange bowls of sugar, lightly whipped cream and an assortment of cordials next to the coffee pot and allow guests to help themselves; or you can prepare one of your "international" coffee specialties for them. Some suggestions:

MEXICAN—Kahlua, brandy and coffee (topped with whipped cream)

IRISH—Irish whisky, brown sugar and coffee (topped with whipped cream and freshly grated nutmeg)

SWISS—coffee topped with whipped cream and a square of Swiss milk chocolate

JAMAICAN—coffee liqueur and coffee (topped with whipped cream and a chocolate coffee bean)

ITALIAN—Amaretto and coffee (topped with whipped cream)

Not Another Cocktail Party: A Menu for 30–50

PARTY DRINKS

*The Hurricane • *Kir *Kir Royale

Champagne • White Wine • Red Wine

TO BE PASSED

*Pissaladière on Puff Pastry • *Canape of Blue Cheese, Endive and Walnut

*Canape of Shrimp on Cucumber • *Hummus in Cherry Tomatoes

AT TABLE

*Roast Fillet of Beef, Sliced to Order • French Bread • Coarse-Grained Mustard

or

Baked Holiday Ham (page 63) on Cheese Biscuits (page 65)

Chicken Liver Pâté (page 35) with Sesame Melba Toast (page 36)

Crabmeat Mousse with Green Goddess Sauce (page 37)

A Variety of Cheeses with Grape Clusters (page 83)

Freshly Made Breads and Assorted Crackers

*Dark Chocolate Honey Torte

or

*Chocolate Mousse in Tiny Cups

By our definition, successful cocktail food has three requirements:

1. It must be finger food that requires no plates or utensils (although cocktail napkins are *de rigueur*).

2. It must be capable of being eaten in one or two dainty bites.

3. It must lead to a broad smile of contentment.

WHAT TO SERVE?

The key to planning a cocktail party menu is variety.

Choose a variety of foods: cheeses, vegetables, meats, fruits, fish, pastry.

Choose a variety of presentation: hot, cold, individual hors d'oeuvres (may be passed), large items that guests serve themselves (e.g., baked ham, cheese platter, pâté).

THE BUTLERED PARTY: Pass drinks on trays. Pass hors d'oeuvres on trays (each hors d'oeuvre deserves its own showcase; don't put four types on one tray). Garnish each tray beautifully. This presentation is very elegant, and nice for a small, unhurried gathering before the theater or a concert.

THE COCKTAIL BUFFET: Set up a sumptuous buffet table of finger foods and/or foods that can be sliced to order and served on little biscuits or bread rounds. Place other foods around the party space. Small dishes at the buffet are optional. Set up one or two bars. This procedure works well for serving large groups and for parties of longer duration. When you offer more substantial foods, such as sliced fillet of beef or baked ham, it can really become a full meal for your guests.

THE GALA COCKTAIL BUFFET: Set up bars, also pass special drinks on trays. Set up a buffet table of cocktail foods with a chef carving at table; also pass beautifully garnished trays of hors d'oeuvres. People can eat and drink as much or as little as they like. This format is currently our most popular type of party. It is especially suited to large groups gathered for festive occasions. Passing food and drink is elegant and also prevents bottlenecks at the buffet and bar.

HOW MUCH FOOD TO SERVE?

• For light cocktail parties of the pretheater or predinner type, plan about eight hors d'oeuvres per person. If you are preparing an assortment of eight items, you will make one of each item per guest.

• For cocktail buffets that may become full meals for some of your guests, double the amounts.

• Certain foods will be party favorites—for example, anything with shrimp, and anything sliced to order at the buffet table—so plan to have more of these items, and less of others.

HOW MUCH HELP?

How much help you need is determined by the method of presentation you choose, the degree of elegance you desire and the amount of money you want to spend. To suggest the range:

For a cocktail party for 30 to 50 you will need a minimum of two in help: one at the bar and one doing everything else.

For absolute elegance, you will need five in help: one at the bar; one passing drinks, bussing glasses, passing food; one at the buffet table, carving; one plating and passing food; and one person taking coats, assisting and cleaning up.

The Hurricane *(A PARTY DRINK)*

This is the kind of rum drink served in hollowed-out pineapples or coconuts at kitschy, pseudo-Hawaiian restaurants. If you leave out the pineapple, the coconut and the ubiquitous paper parasol, this is a delicious and colorful party drink. (If you like kitsch, by all means go the parasol route.)

3 ounces orange juice
1 ounce Rose's Lime Juice
1 teaspoon superfine sugar
Dash Grenadine
1½ ounces dark rum, or
   rum of choice
Ice cubes
½ slice orange, maraschino
   cherry with stem

Pour all the ingredients into a 12-ounce glass *filled* with ice cubes. Stir thoroughly and decorate with the orange slice and maraschino cherry.

NOTE: The juice mixture—everything except the rum—may be mixed ahead in quantity following the same proportions. When serving, use 4½ ounces of the mixture per drink, add the rum, stir well and decorate.

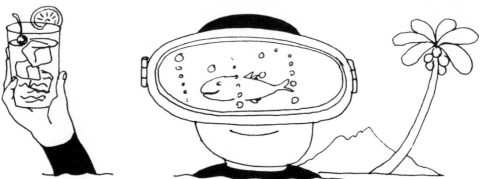

Kir and Kir Royale *(PARTY DRINKS)*

These drinks look spectacular on a tray being passed among your guests, especially if you opt for the fresh strawberry decoration. Kir is white wine with a splash of Crème de Cassis, a liqueur made from black currants. Kir Royale is its rich cousin: champagne with a splash of Crème de Cassis.

Dry white wine or champagne,
   well chilled
Crème de Cassis, to taste
Fresh strawberry or strip of
   lemon peel

Because these drinks are so much a matter of taste, we are not giving you a recipe—only the method. Fill a tulip-shaped wine glass half full with dry white wine or champagne. Add a dash of Crème de Cassis, or to taste (remembering, of course, that Cassis is thick, sweet and syrupy and it is not sophisticated to wind up with soda pop). Purists may shudder, but in summer these drinks may be served on ice.

NOTE: Brands of Crème de Cassis vary considerably in quality, density and richness of taste, so ask your wine merchant to recommend a good one.

Pissaladiere on Puff Pastry

Makes 48 pieces

This is our nontraditional bite-sized version of an onion/anchovy/olive pizza popular in the South of France. Rather than use whole strips of anchovy on top (which automatically divides the world into lovers and haters), we mince the anchovy with the onion for a more subtle effect. We also use rounds of puff pastry instead of a heavier pizza dough.

8 well-chilled rounds puff pastry (see Note)
1½ pounds onions, thinly sliced
3 tablespoons clarified butter (see page 23)
2-ounce can anchovies in olive oil, drained (with oil reserved), and finely chopped
About 2 ounces canned chopped black olives (or chop whole ones yourself)
Flour to dust pastry board and rolling pin
Garnish: parsley sprigs, ½ lemon, decoratively cut

If you are using frozen pastry rounds, defrost them. Cook the onions in the butter over high heat until brown but not crisp. Remove from the heat. Add the anchovy oil to the onions and cook over moderate heat for about 3 minutes, stirring to combine. Add the chopped anchovies and mix well. Remove from the heat and cool. Drain the olives, discarding the liquid.

Preheat the oven to 450 degrees and position the racks in the upper third of the oven. Have 2 non-stick baking sheets ready. Roll out the puff pastry on a lightly floured cloth or board to make 5-inch circles, about 3/16 inch thick. Spread 1 heaping tablespoon of the onion mixture evenly over each pastry circle, leaving a small border (about 3/16 inch) of pastry showing, and then sprinkle a heaping 1/2 teaspoon chopped olives on top of the onion on each one. Place the circles on the baking sheets, using a spatula. (If you are baking one sheet at a time, refrigerate the second sheet until ready to bake.) Bake until the pastry borders are puffed and brown (about 15 to 20 minutes).

Transfer the hot circles to a cutting board. Cutting straight down with a chef's knife, cut each one in half and then cut each half into 3 small pie-shaped wedges. (You should have 6 wedges per circle.) To serve, arrange the wedges in a neat ring with the pastry crusts barely touching and the tips pointing into the center of the tray. Garnish the platter with a decoratively cut half lemon resting on a bed of parsley. Serve at once.

NOTE: The best puff pastry is that which you make yourself. However, several commercially prepared puff pastry doughs are available in markets around the country. We find most of them unsuitable for use in desserts owing to their lack of butter and oily aftertaste, but acceptable in savory dishes such as this one. Pepperidge Farm Pastry Rounds are the most readily available.

Canape of Blue Cheese, Endive and Walnut

Makes about 72 pieces

This is one of the simplest, and yet most elegant, hors d'oeuvres. Many caterers use endive leaves as "canoes" to transport interesting fillings, but for some reason they use the whole leaf. People bite off the filling at one end and don't know where to dock the rest. It's much nicer to use just the tips of the leaves and to enjoy the rest of the endive in a salad the next day. If Belgian endive is unavailable, substitute a thin round of young cucumber (but then don't serve shrimp on cucumber as well).

1 pound cream cheese, at room temperature
½ pound blue cheese, at room temperature
4 tablespoons unsalted butter, at room temperature
1 clove garlic, well mashed
6 drops Tabasco sauce
3-4 tablespoons heavy cream
12 Belgian endives
Garnish: 72 walnut halves, toasted in a 350-degree oven and cooled to room temperature

Beat the cream cheese, blue cheese and butter in the bowl of an electric mixer until light and fluffy. Add the garlic and Tabasco sauce and beat well. Add the cream, as needed, to thin the mixture slightly. Refrigerate for at least 30 minutes.

Cut through each endive, about 3 inches from the pointed tip, and reserve the stem ends of the endive for use elsewhere. Separate the leaf tips from one another and carefully wash and dry them. Put the cheese mixture in a pastry bag fitted with a star tube. Holding each leaf tip in turn by the point, pipe a cheese rosette at the broad end. Top the rosette with a walnut half. Arrange the endive leaves on a serving tray in concentric circles, with the tips pointing outward. They will resemble flower petals. Place a fresh flower at the center of the tray, if you like, and serve.

NOTE: The cheese mixture may be made several days ahead and refrigerated. To serve, return to room temperature and whisk (or re-whip) until smooth.

If there are leftovers from this canape, combine the cheese mixture with chopped walnuts, spoon into crocks and serve with Sesame Melba Toast (see page 36).

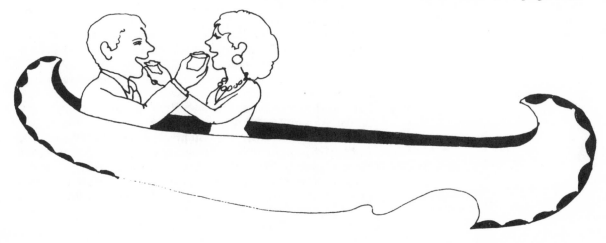

Canape of Shrimp on Cucumber

Makes 60-64 pieces

Shrimp is invariably the most popular item at any cocktail party. There are many different ways of serving it, among them: sushi, tempura, fritters and, of course, peeled and served au naturel *with spicy red cocktail sauce or Green Goddess Sauce (page 38). This canape is one of our favorite presentations. The crisp cucumber and zippy mayonnaise complement the shrimp beautifully, and the red pickled ginger adds unexpected taste and color. Don't try to be generous and put a whole shrimp on each slice of cucumber. They stay in place better when sliced in half, and make the canape much easier to eat.*

½ lemon
Large pinch salt
1½ pounds fresh unshelled shrimp (medium-size: 20-24 to a pound)
¼-½ cup mayonnaise
Prepared horseradish sauce, to taste
4 thin seedless hothouse cucumbers, washed and dried
Garnish: Japanese red pickled ginger, cut into ¼-inch dots, or flat-leafed Italian parsley, separated into tiny leaves

Bring about 6 quarts of water to a rapid boil in an 8-quart saucepan. Squeeze the lemon into the water, adding the rind and a generous pinch of salt. Add the shrimp, stir and return to a boil. Turn off the heat and let the shrimp sit in the hot water until just cooked through (test after 3 minutes). Plunge the cooked shrimp into cold water to stop the cooking. Drain. Peel and devein them, removing the tails. Slice each one in half horizontally, from middle to tail. Trim any raggedy edges and arrange the shrimp neatly on a plate. Cover and refrigerate until ready to assemble the canape.

Flavor the mayonnaise to taste with horseradish sauce. It should be zippy, but not bitingly hot. Refrigerate.

Using a zester, lightly score 8 to 12 strips along the length of the cucumber. Cut it, slightly on the diagonal to fit the size of the shrimp, into ¼-inch-thick slices. If you are not making the canape immediately, reassemble the cucumber by stacking the slices together, seal with plastic wrap and refrigerate.

To assemble the canape, place the cucumber slices on paper towels to drain, if necessary. Blot dry. Spread a small dab of horseradish mayonnaise over each slice of cucumber, not quite to the edge, and then position a shrimp half, cut side down, over that. Ideally, the curve of the shrimp will fit the curve of the cucumber. Place a ¼-inch dot of red pickled ginger at the center of each and serve.

NOTE: You cannot use mature, heavily seeded cucumbers for this recipe. Look for the new variety of seedless cucumbers and select ones that are firm, green and uniform in width. Red pickled ginger (*beni shoga*) is available in Oriental and specialty stores. If you buy the type that is already cut into strips, you need only drain a few strips and cut them into ¼-inch pieces. Store the remainder in the refrigerator.

Don't make this canape too far ahead. The cucumber will give off moisture and everything else will slip off.

Hummus in Cherry Tomatoes

Makes 48 pieces

This pungent and aromatic hors d'oeuvre is a Middle Eastern recipe. If you make the hummus mixture a few hours ahead, drizzle a little olive oil over the top to prevent a crust from forming, then cover and refrigerate until ready to use. Don't make the mixture the day before; it will lose all subtleties of flavor.

To make hors d'oeuvres like these look professional, you must use a piping bag to fill the tomatoes, but if you use a small spoon, they will taste just as good.

48 small ripe cherry tomatoes, stems removed
2 cloves garlic
1 teaspoon salt, or to taste
2 20-ounce cans chick peas, drained and juice reserved
½ cup lemon juice
1 cup tahini (sesame paste); available in specialty stores
2 tablespoons olive oil
Garnish: flat-leafed Italian parsley, separated into 48 tiny leaves

Carefully remove the seeds and pulp from the tomatoes with a demitasse spoon (or you may turn them upside down and squeeze gently). Place upside down on paper towels to drain.

Drop the garlic and salt through the feed tube of a food processor fitted with a steel blade and process until finely chopped. Measure 2 cups chick peas, add them to the food processor and process to blend. Add the lemon juice and then the tahini, processing to blend after each. Add the oil through the feed tube and process to make a smooth puree. If the puree is too thick to pipe from a piping bag, blend in some of the reserved chick pea juice, little by little, until the proper consistency is attained.

Transfer the hummus to a piping bag fitted with a small star tube. Fill the tomatoes with the mixture, garnishing the top of each rosette with a leaf of parsley.

Roast Fillet of Beef

This is one of the most expensive hors d'oeuvres you can serve; it is also one of the most delicious and impressive. If you use a thin-bladed carving knife to slice each meltingly tender beef fillet, you should be able to carve about 40 very thin rounds. However, that does not mean you will serve 40 people per fillet; guests will certainly have more than one canape each. For 50 guests, it's wise to prepare 3 fillets. (In for a penny, in for a pound!)

3 4-pound beef fillets, trimmed and tied (by you or a butcher), removed from refrigerator about 30 minutes prior to roasting

MUSTARD COATING:
3 tablespoons coarse-grained mustard
1½ tablespoons peanut oil
1½ tablespoons melted butter
1½ teaspoons dried thyme, crushed
3 small cloves garlic, finely chopped
2 tablespoons soy sauce

Preheat the oven to 450 degrees. Whisk together all the ingredients for the mustard coating in a bowl until blended. Rub the coating into the fillets with your fingers and place them in a shallow roasting pan, large enough to hold all 3 without touching. Place the pan in the upper third of the oven and roast for 15 minutes. Reduce the temperature to 350 degrees and, checking the internal temperature every 5 minutes, roast until a meat thermometer registers a temperature of 125 degrees (for rare beef).

Remove from the oven and let rest at room temperature for at least 20 minutes before carving. The beef may be served warm or at room temperature. To serve, place on a cutting board (with a lip if possible). Remove the strings and slice into thin rounds, placing each one onto a slice of French bread, cut slightly on the diagonal. Serve with coarse-grained mustard or horseradish mayonnaise.

NOTE: You may prepare these canapes a few minutes ahead, but it is much more fun if you can carve to order during the party. If you wish to serve the beef warm, slice one fillet at a time at the table, keeping the others in a warm oven until needed. Cover them lightly with foil, but do not seal.

Dark Chocolate Honey Nut Torte

The most difficult part of this recipe may be locating the oblaten torten—*thin, crisp unsweetened wafers (a.k.a.* gaufrettes*), which are usually available at German and specialty stores. A chocolate filling is spread between these wafers, to make what looks like a giant candy bar, but tastes even better. Make the torte a week or two ahead, if desired. It keeps beautifully without refrigeration.*

¾ pound unsalted butter
1¼ cups sugar
1 cup honey
¾ pound walnuts, coarsely
  ground
¼ pound unsweetened baking
  chocolate, coarsely chopped
1 tablespoon Dutch process
  cocoa powder
1 tablespoon dark rum
2 tablespoons instant espresso
6-8 9-inch squares unsweetened
  oblaten torten (pastry wafers)

Bring the butter, sugar and honey to a boil in a large saucepan over low heat, stirring constantly. Add the walnuts, baking chocolate and cocoa powder and stir for 5 minutes. Remove from the heat. Gradually blend in the dark rum (be careful, the mixture may froth) and the 2 tablespoons instant espresso.

Place a wafer, pattern side up, on a platter. Working quickly so the filling does not become too firm, smoothly spread about ½ cup filling over the top to the edges. Place another wafer over the chocolate layer, pattern side down. Firmly press in place with both hands held flat over the wafer. Spread the top with another layer of chocolate filling, and top with another wafer. Repeat with the remaining wafers, pattern sides down. Spread the remaining chocolate smoothly over the top and sides of the torte, spreading the chocolate up the sides as the torte cools. Let stand at room temperature for at least a day before serving.

To serve, use a long thin serrated knife to cut the torte into 4 equal rectangles. Cut each rectangle into 18 ½-inch-thick slices, arrange them decoratively on a platter and serve. The guests will eat them as finger food, so you will not need separate plates.

Chocolate Mousse

Serves 25

This dark chocolate mousse is actually improved by being made a day or two ahead, because the flavors develop. To serve 50, repeat the recipe; the mousse can be frozen without losing quality.

1½ pounds semi- or bittersweet chocolate, coarsely chopped
½ pound unsweetened baking
  chocolate, coarsely chopped
2 cups heavy cream, well chilled
12 large eggs, separated and
  at room temperature
1 cup plus 2 tablespoons
  superfine sugar
6 tablespoons Cognac
3 tablespoons strong coffee,
  at room temperature

Melt all the chocolate in the top of a double boiler over hot (but not boiling) water. Remove and let cool. Meanwhile, whip the cream in a bowl until stiff. Beat the yolks with the sugar in a separate large bowl until light and fluffy, and mix in the Cognac and coffee. Beat the whites in another large bowl until stiff but not dry. Gently fold the cooled chocolate into the yolk mixture, then fold in the whites. Fold in the cream. Cover and refrigerate until 1 hour before serving.

No-Effort Parties

Sometimes, the idea of feeding a crowd of people just seems too much to handle. Occasions like this, which often arise spontaneously, are best handled by serving platters of cheeses with freshly baked breads or assorted crackers (see opposite page), or by visiting the take-out shops that are springing up in every major city in the country and a surprising number of places in between. If there is one in your vicinity, ask for the menu of take-out selections. Just looking at the list of possibilities will surely whet your appetite, and give you some good ideas.

Why not buy some, and make some yourself? A few suggestions:

• A julienne of smoked deli meats tossed in mayonnaise with capers, chopped pickle and fresh apple slices
• Fingers of honeydew melon (or other ripe, firm melon) and prosciutto; or wedges of fresh pineapple with prosciutto; or prosciutto and fresh figs
• Thin slices of ham wrapped around asparagus spears, cooked al dente
• More of the al dente asparagus (or string beans) brushed with Oriental Dressing (sesame oil, soy sauce, white vinegar, a dash of sugar and a dash of salt), garnished with toasted sesame seeds
• Canned smoked mussels, clams or oysters, drained and tossed in a mustard mayonnaise with chopped shallots or scallions and plenty of minced parsley
• An antipasto salad

• A tomato and mozzarella salad—for when you have red, ripe tomatoes. Alternate slices of tomato with fresh (and/or smoked) mozzarella cheese, garnish with chopped fresh basil and dress with a vinaigrette made with virgin olive oil
• An alternative mozzarella salad—slices of mozzarella cheese topped with sun-dried tomatoes and drizzled with virgin olive oil
• Breast of chicken salad, made with poached breast of chicken cut into large cubes and combined with chopped celery, dressed with mayonnaise flavored with dried tarragon and a splash of tarragon vinegar, garnished with thin slivers of fresh pineapple or rounds of fresh orange
• On the grill: Boned and butterflied leg of lamb marinated in red wine, olive oil and herbs from Provence
• Assorted German wursts: weisswurst, knockwurst, bratwurst, served on cheese biscuits, with a variety of pickles and mustards
• Salad of fresh orange and onion—oranges peeled and sliced into rounds, scattered with rings of purple onion, and dressed with vinaigrette
• Cold pasta salads—morsels of fresh seasonal vegetables cooked al dente with various kinds of pasta (larger, macaroni types such as ziti are best if you are buying dried pasta; or you can purchase freshly made pastas, or make your own), in a sauce vinaigrette; add cooked and cubed duck, chicken or beef to make into a main course dish

A Note on Cheeses

From supermarket to shopping mall, from gourmet store to deli, America has discovered the cheese shop. We can now serve our party guests a resplendent spread of cheeses instead of the ubiquitous cheese spreads of yore. But this very abundance from which to choose creates its own problems of selection.

Here are a few suggestions about selecting and presenting cheeses:

• Before you select a cheese, decide when and how you plan to serve it. Will it be a spreadable hors d'oeuvre (not our favorite!) offered as a selection on the buffet table; or an accompaniment to the salad course; or with fresh fruit, or with savories such as black olives?

• Only buy cheese at the peak of flavor and texture. Be a discriminating customer and request information about cheeses you are not familiar with; ask to taste. It is better to buy one perfect cheese than any number of imperfect ones.

• It is also acceptable to serve one cheese rather than many: a circle of perfectly ripe Corolle or St. André or Brie, for example, surrounded by small clusters of grapes (cut to size with scissors), makes a beautiful and delicious presentation.

• When selecting cheeses for an assortment, consider contrast in taste, texture and appearance, and also consider the tastes of your guests. For example, you might choose:

One soft cheese which is creamy and mild, such as Brie, Reblochon, Camembert

One soft goat's milk cheese, either pungent (a cylinder of Ste.-Maure) or mild (a pyramid of Valençay)

One blue-veined cheese, such as Bleu de Bresse or Roquefort, cut in a wedge

One very pungent cheese, such as Pont-L'Evêque or Époisses

One hard cheese: Jarlsberg, Comté

• Surprise your guests. Choose at least one cheese that you think will be completely new to them, and learn something about it from your supplier so you can answer questions (and impress your guests with your savoir faire).

• Make certain that you know and record the names of all the cheeses you serve so that you can remember the popular ones for your next party.

Presenting Cheese

The most important consideration in serving cheese is to have it at the proper temperature—it is often served too cold. For a buffet, we suggest you assemble your cheese tray(s) about an hour before the party, cover with plastic wrap and place on the table.

Serve a butter knife with each kind of cheese offered and accompany with unsalted crackers that have a neutral flavor, or breadsticks, or crisp French bread.

Fresh fruits that make an attractive and tasty accompaniment for cheeses include grapes, figs, strawberries, pears, apples and kumquats.

Tortellini Primavera *(COLD PASTA AND VEGETABLE SALAD)* *Serves 24*

Pasta has been called the bread of the 80s. Its versatility is astounding. It can be served hot or cold, and dressed with everything from peanut butter (as in Chinese sesame noodles) to vegetables in a sprightly vinaigrette—our choice for a colorful and festive party dish.

Our room-temperature salad is also extremely versatile. We use fresh green and yellow tortellini— purchased from a take-out food shop—as the pasta; but you can certainly substitute any pasta you like, as well as your own choice of vegetables. To turn this dish into a hearty main course, add about 4 pounds cooked diced ham or chicken; or rounds of both sweet and hot Italian sausage.

1 dozen asparagus spears, or snow pea pods, cut into fine julienne
2 bunches broccoli, cut into florets
3 pounds spinach tortellini, cooked al dente
3 pounds yellow tortellini, cooked al dente
1½ cups Creamy Vinaigrette Dressing (see page 26)
Chopped fresh basil, or chopped Italian parsley, to taste
2 green peppers, seeded and diced
2 yellow peppers, seeded and diced
2 red peppers, seeded and diced
3 carrots, peeled and cut into fine julienne
3 scallions, cut into rings
1 yellow squash, seeded but not peeled, cut into fine julienne
2 zucchini squash, seeded but not peeled, cut into fine julienne
Salt, to taste
White pepper, to taste

Blanch the broccoli and asparagus, then immediately fan to cool.

Toss the pasta and dressing and two-thirds of the vegetables in a large bowl. Taste for seasoning. Garnish with the remaining vegetables just before serving. Serve at cool room temperature.